John Samut Tagliaferro

MALTA
ITS ARCHAEOLOGY AND HISTORY

■ **Miller Distributors Limited**
Miller House, Tarxien Road, Airport Way, Luqa Malta.
P.O. Box 25 Malta International Airport LQA 05
Telephone: 664488 Facsimile: 676799
MILLER

Published and printed by

NARNI - TERNI

*"This book is dedicated
to the memory of the late Francis Miller,
founder of the co-publishing company,
who had a great love for Malta's rich history."*

INDEX

Kevin Casha and Impact Photographic Services are synonymous with image creativity, quality and innovation.

With years of intensive involvement and experience behind him, Kevin has successfully tackled virtually every facet of photography. From Advertising to Portraiture, from Industrial to Landscape, right through to Aerial photography. His constant striving for perfection, dedication and love of photography, coupled with reliability, has won him many long-standing clients.

Four times Malta's Photographer of the Year, Kevin has won all awards local Photography has to offer. He is also Chairman of the Malta Institute of Professional Photography, an organisation he was instrumental in setting up and establishing.

His work has been exhibited regularly both locally and abroad, in places like Italy, U.S.A. and France, whilst his most recent Exhibition, "15 Years of photography" was a resounding success, both for content, as well as for the innovative manner in which it was presented.

© Copyright by CASA EDITRICE PLURIGRAF
S.S. Flaminia, km 90 - 05035 NARNI - TERNI - ITALIA
Tel. 0744 / 715946 - Fax 0744 / 722540 - (Italy country code: +39)
All rights reserved. No Part of this publication may be reproduced.
Printed: 2000 - PLURIGRAF S.p.A. - NARNI

PREHISTORY

1. GEOLOGICAL FORMATION

In geological terms the Maltese Islands are relatively young. The rocks comprising Malta's stratigraphy were laid down in a marine environment between approximately 25 to 5 million years ago.

When one considers that the rocks in Greenland are about 3800 million years old, then Malta is indeed of recent origin.

Malta's rocks are sedimentary (there are no igneous or metamorphic deposits), and they were laid down in an essentially lagoonal environment at various depths and distances from the existing land mass in the Oligocene and Miocene epochs of the Tertiary period.

The precise environment and timing in which the rocks were laid down determines their composition or lithology, and it results that Malta's stratigraphy is made up of five main layers.

These are, from above downwards:

1. Upper Coralline Limestone

2. Greensand/ Sandstone

3. Blue Clay

4. Globigerina Limestone

5. Lower Coralline Limestone

In scattered areas of the Islands, such as below the Fort Chambray

promontory in Gozo, a thin superficial Quaternary deposit can also be found.

The limestones were laid down at a greater depth and distance from the continental land mass than the greensand layer, which was deposited in a transitional coastal environment.

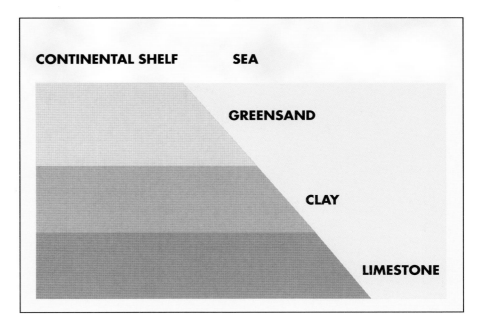

Victoria lines.

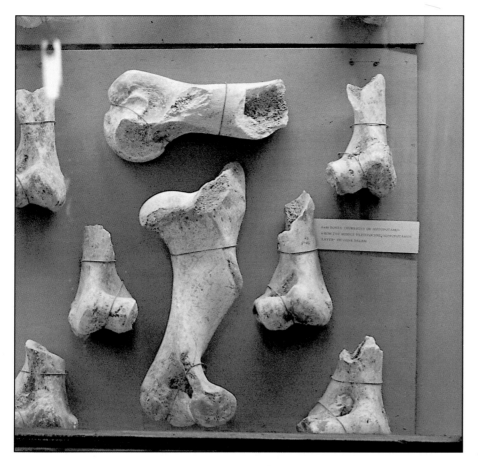

Ghar Dalam Museum.

Originally laid down in horizontal layers, the earth's tectonic movements and continental shifts forced this land mass above the surface of the sea and created the Maltese Islands. In various places the horizontal layers can be seen to have been tilted and bent, and there are also fault lines where the earth has slipped. The most spectacular of these is the Great Fault which traverses the main island of Malta from Ras ir-Raheb in the west to Madliena in the east. The escarpment created by this fault was utilised for defensive purposes by the British in the nineteenth century when they constructed the Victoria Lines along its ridge.

The topography of the Maltese Islands, as well as their flora and architectural appearance, have been determined by the five main stratigraphical layers. Weathering and erosion has formed hilltops capped by upper coralline limestone which are found principally in Gozo and in the northern part of Malta, whereas the flatter southern part of Malta is mainly composed of globigerina limestone.

The surface limestone, which comprises the bulk of Malta's topography, is particularly susceptible to chemical weathering caused by acids in the rainfall. Where the surface is formed of coralline limestone it is rendered furrowed and fretted by the irregular solvent action of acids. This is the typical KARST erosion seen to good effect on the lower coralline rocks by the Salina coast road in Malta. Weathering of the softer globigerina limestone, on the other hand, tends to be of a more flaky and crumbling nature.

The coralline limestone has a hard, compact and crystalline composition, and is a first class building material, utilised in the more important buildings in Malta. It is known locally as *tal-qawwi* or *zonqor*.

The greensand layer, however, is friable and not suitable as a building material. Its prime importance lies in the fact that it is porous and it overlies the impermeable clay layer. Rain water that percolates down through the upper layers is trapped in this layer, forming the reservoir for the surface water table. It has been tapped by local farmers since time immemorial who sink shafts down to this level. Water used to be drawn up by mule-driven water mills, though these have now been superceded by mechanical pumps. In areas where these layers have been eroded and are exposed, natural springs are thrown out by the underlying impermeable clay bed.

This supply of water, together with that from the lower water table (a fresh water body mass floating on a saturated zone of salt water in the form of a lens) has long been the mainstay of local farmers. But the low annual rainfall, the growth of the resident population, and particularly the development of the tourism and manufacturing industries has meant that the demand for fresh water has far outstripped its natural supply in recent years. The problem was addressed by the establishment of reverse osmosis plants. The bulk of Malta's fresh water supply is now obtained from this technology, (the conversion of sea water to fresh water), but not without financial and political cost. The provision of this scarce commodity is a severe drain on government's finances and the high water and electricity rates passed on to the local consumer to pay for this costly technology are

Ghar Dalam Cave.

generally held to be one of the principal factors contributing to the failure of the Government to be re-elected in the 1998 elections.

The globigerina limestone horizon has supplied most of Malta's building material since earliest times and is the Islands' most abundant natural resource. It has even been exported; Government House in Corfu was built with Maltese stone. It is responsible for the appearance of the Islands' man-made landscape, since most of the buildings, fortifications, and field rubble walls are derived from this layer. Known locally as *franka*, it is a pale yellow soft limestone, easily worked and quarried. It turns a rosy or warm brownish colour when exposed to the atmosphere, which is a protective skin or patina. However, it is of variable quality and durability, as can be ascertained from casual observation of Malta's buildings. Some stones exhibit a honeycomb-like weathering pattern on their surface in a relatively short time, whereas the more durable stone from better quality quarries may

survive for thousands of years, as evidenced in the Punic building at Zurrieq.

Towards the evening the limestone buildings take on a characteristic pinkish hue. It is a sign of the times that globigerina limestone is gradually being replaced in the local building industry by prefabricated blockrete cement blocks.

Malta's geological strata are distinguished not only by their lithological differences, described above, but also by the different fossils they contain. As each stratum was laid down in a different palaeoenvironment, i.e. at different times and at varying depths below the sea and distance from the coast, so they contain different animal and plant fossils. These can be seen exposed in numerous places in rocks all over

the Maltese Islands as well as in the cut stones of the buildings.

A word of caution here. Fossils are protected by law through the Antiquities (Protection) Act which prohibits the exportation of geological and palaeontological material.

If any fossils surface in your luggage on departure your travel plans and pocket may be severely disrupted.

As Malta lies between the oilfields of North Africa and Sicily, high hopes are entertained of finding oil in Maltese waters. A recent exploratory borehole drilled to a depth of some 8,000 metres at a site in Gozo is currently undergoing evaluation as to the economic viability of oil or natural gas extraction from this area.

The latest indications suggest that it may not be a viable well.

2. THE ICE AGES

During the Ice Ages, the last of which ended approximately 12,000 years ago, the Maltese landmass and Sicily were connected via their respective south-eastern extremities. When an Ice Age occurs a significant amount of sea water is incorporated into the polar ice masses which results in a drop in sea level. Conversely, when the ice melts in an interglacial period, the sea level rises, and that is what happened about 12,000 years ago, isolating the Maltese Islands as separate entities in the Mediterranean down to the present day.

During an Ice Age the landbridge that existed with Sicily permitted the migration of animals southwards to the warmer land mass that now comprises the Maltese Islands. Cold-intolerant animals were pushed down by the southward creeping ice sheets on the European continent.

The Ice Age left its impact on Malta not only in the kind of animals that inhabited it, but also by shaping its very topography. The Maltese climate in those days would have been much wetter, resembling more the climate of present day northern Europe. The Maltese landmass would have been much greener and covered by woodland. The heavy rains would have been responsible for carving up the landscape and forming the valleys as we know them today. Underground caverns and caves were also hollowed out. One such cave is that of Ghar Dalam, situated in the southern part of Malta near Birzebbugia. It is a good example of the KARST phenomenon erosive process within the lower coralline limestone layer, and it is Malta's most important palaeontological site, well worth a visit. It is about 145 metres long, and its prime importance lies in the fact that within it was found a sequence of fossilised deposits of animals extending back from about 130,000 years ago down to modern times. These deposits record the animal

Ghar Dalam cave.

history of Ice Age Malta, and they illustrate the effect of prolonged insular conditions on the local fauna during an interglacial period. They show evidence of the sudden introduction of new animals via the temporary establishment of landbridges with Sicily during an Ice Age, and how they evolved locally when the ice melted and isolated the Maltese Islands. During a warm interglacial period of isolation the animals survived by becoming stunted and dwarfed, and fine examples of the fossilised bones of extinct Maltese pygmy elephants and dwarf hippopotami are on show at the Ghar Dalam Museum adjacent to the cave. Within the cave the lower hippopotamus layer also contains the bones of several types of dwarf elephant as well as extinct species of dormice, bats and avian remains, and probably dates to about 125,000 years ago.

The more recent upper cervus layer, possibly dating from about 18,000 years ago, contains abundant remains of the stunted forms of the European Red Deer. Scanty remains of carnivores in the form of a small-sized brown bear, red fox and wolf have also been found in the deer layer, along with the remains of bats, voles, birds, turtles and amphibians.

The uppermost cultural or domestic animal layer shows definite evidence of human presence dating from about 5,200 B.C. down to the present century.

Fragmentary human skeletal remains have also been found in Ghar Dalam. It is a vexed question whether some of these may belong to palaeolithic man who could have been hunting these ice age animals in Malta.

There is abundant indisputable evidence for palaeolithic man in Sicily at a time when present day Sicily and Malta formed part of one contiguous land mass. It is almost inconceivable, therefore, that palaeolithic man would not also have extended his wanderings down to the warmer tip of this land mass, Malta, only some 100 km further south.

In 1917 two human taurodont (bullteeth) molars were discovered at Ghar Dalam, and it was claimed that these could only belong to Neanderthal man. But subsequently, in the 1960's, tens of thousands of years of Maltese history were wiped out when published relative dating tests on the Ghar Dalam taurodonts suggested that they belonged to Neolithic (post 5,000 B.C.) and not to Neanderthal man (approx. 125,000 - 25,000 B.C.). It was also pointed out that taurodonts occur in modern humans as well.

New claims emerged in the late 1980's when it was proposed that palaeolithic cave paintings had been discovered in Ghar Hassan on the south-east coast, and it has also been suggested that palaeolithic tools have been found in Malta. Although the presence of palaeolithic man in Malta seems highly likely, tangible bodily proof of this presence has yet to find universal acceptance. More reliable modern scientific absolute dating methods applied to the human skeletal remains should help solve the issue one way or the other.

3. NEOLITHIC MALTA (5,200 - 4,100 B.C.)

I) GHAR DALAM PHASE
(5,200 - 4,500 B.C.)

The earliest undisputed evidence of man's presence in Malta dates to about 5,200 B.C., and this evidence relates to radiocarbon dating of material from Skorba. This does not in any way exclude man's presence earlier; this evidence merely represents the earliest traces of man in Malta that have happened to survive and that we have happened to come across and that have been satisfactorily dated. Much in archaeology rests on chance, and the chances are that one day this date will be pushed back. I have already referred to the likelihood of palaeolithic hunting man's presence in Malta.

But that of which there is no doubt is that some time after the end of the last ice age an intrepid new group of Neolithic immigrant farmers arrived on Maltese shores. From whence did they come? The pottery brought over by these immigrants, known as impressed ware, bears close resemblance with that of the Stentinello and Monte Kronio cultures of South Sicily, from where Malta can be seen on a clear day. These Sicilians brought with them not only their families, equipment and tools, but also their domestic livestock and cereals to cultivate the land. This daring sea voyage in primitive craft marked the arrival of the agricultural revolution to the Maltese Islands, and evidence of this people's culture was found in the upper layers of Ghar Dalam cave, the site which gave its name to this first phase of Maltese prehistory. Ghar Dalam phase pottery has also been found in a cave in Gozo known as *Il-Mixta*. Being the northernmost island of the Maltese group, it is likely that these first immigrants initially landed on Gozo, probably beaching in the north-eastern bays of Marsalforn and Ramla.

II) GREY AND RED SKORBA
PHASES (4,500 - 4,100 B.C.)

The subsequent two phases of the Neolithic period are named after the site in Malta (Skorba), which was excavated by David Trump, and where the development of the decorated Ghar Dalam pottery was first noticed. The impressed ware with incised geometric decorations was replaced by undecorated pottery of a dull grey colour (Grey Skorba 4,500 - 4,400 B.C.), and after a century or so this same pottery was given a red slip or coating (Red Skorba 4,400 - 4,100 B.C.). This red slipped pottery, together with its characteristic angular shapes, lugs and horn or M-shape handled ladles, bears close resemblance to the pottery of the contemporary Diana culture of the islands of Sicily and Lipari.

It is clear that cultural and economic ties continued to be maintained between Malta and Sicily throughout the Neolithic period.
The raw materials man needed to make his cutting and pointed tools were not available in Malta's sedimentary layers. Flint was imported from Sicily, and the valuable and highly prized black obsidian stone was obtained from the volcanic islands of Lipari and Pantelleria, probably via Sicily.

These early Neolithic farmers lived in caves and rock shelters, though there is also evidence that they constructed mud-brick or wattle and daub huts on low stone foundations floored with clay. Indications of their religious beliefs survive in the form of fragments of several female figurines found at Skorba in what appears to have been a shrine.
These may represent the earliest evidence in Malta of the cult of a female divinity.
These figurines, in which the female sex characteristics are pronounced, constitute the first representations of the human form in Malta. Other than the one in stone, all are made of pottery.

4. THE TEMPLE PERIOD (4,100 - 2,500 B.C.)

The turn of the fourth millennium B.C. marks the beginning of the second period of Maltese prehistory, the Temple Period, during which those awe-inspiring and unique megalithic structures were built.
It corresponds to the Copper Age on mainland Europe, though there is no evidence of this metallurgical technology in the Malta of that time.

I) ZEBBUG PHASE
(4,100 - 3,800 B.C.)

The Temple Period is ushered in by the Zebbug phase where it seems a new wave of Sicilian immigrants introduce a new type of pottery to Malta, which bears similarities to the San Cono-Piano Notaro/Grotta Zubbia Sicilian cultures. The shape, structure and decoration of the pottery differ markedly from that of the preceding Skorba phase. The characteristic pear-shaped jar has curvilinear incised or painted decoration, and the clay is of a dark mottled or yellowish buff colour.

The most significant development of this phase however, is that for the first time in Malta there is evidence of man burying his dead in intentionally prepared and cut tombs. We do not know how man disposed of his dead in Malta before this time. Zebbug (Malta) is the type site which first provided the evidence for these collective burials in artificial rock-cut tombs, and in 1988 a Zebbug phase two-chambered tomb served by a central shaft was discovered at the edge of the Brochtorff Circle (Xaghra, Gozo) site, analysis of which has significantly added to our understanding of this early form of mortuary ritual in Malta.

The bones of a minimum of fifty-four adults and eleven children have been identified in this tomb; both males and females, as well as adults and children of a range of ages being represented. Most of the bones were disarticulated and pushed to the back and sides of the chambers, as if to make way for a more recent burial. Indeed, at the entrance of one of the chambers lay the contracted almost complete skeleton of an adult male, presumably the last of the burials.

Artefacts deposited in the tomb with a ritual and symbolic significance include pottery, worked limestone, greenstone, obsidian, chert and flint objects, as well as artefacts made from mollusc or fossil shells and from animal bones. Much red ochre was also found, its blood colour associating it with the death ritual. The objects included axes, blades and flakes, pendants, buttons, beads, querns, rubbers, hammerstones and mixing palettes. Of particular interest is the 17cm "statue menhir" globigerina limestone idol found just inside the entrance of the tomb. This highly stylised almost abstract human representation differs in function and appearance from the earlier Skorba figurines and the "Mother Goddesses" that were to follow. This Gozitan idol (like its Maltese counterpart at Ta' Trapna, Zebbug) had a funerary function. It is thought that it may have acted as guardian of the tomb, and perhaps even as a tomb marker, as it is conceivable that its original position may have been exterior to the tomb.

This tomb remained in use for many centuries, (one chamber was used into the early Ġgantija Phase), probably by succeeding generations of the same kin, and when mortuary practice evolved it was sealed with a large circular stone slab.

Other early evidence of mortuary ritual in Malta comes from the ossiferous fissure burial cave of Bur Mghez discovered in 1911 by Professor Napoleon Tagliaferro. It contained well over one hundred individuals and a considerable quantity of animal bones, principally those of deer. Some of the human bones appeared to have been disarticulated and piled in heaps during the time the cave was used for burial, in order to make room for later bodies. These were

Mġarr Temple.

Mġarr Temple.

the Temple Period, (and a few even to the Bronze Age), it cannot be excluded that this cave was also in use before that time.

II) MĠARR PHASE
(3,800 - 3,600 B.C.)

This is a transitional phase named after the site in Malta where a development in style of the Zebbug pottery was first noticed.
Shapes are less varied and simpler, and the decoration is composed of broader incised bands which are generally curved.

III) GĠANTIJA PHASE
(3,600 - 3,000 B.C.)

This phase marks a watershed in Maltese prehistory, for this is when the first temples were erected.
They are unique in many ways, not least because they are the earliest free-standing stone monuments built by man extant anywhere in the world. They pre-date the pyramids of Egypt and are older than England's Stonehenge.

mostly laid on their left side in a crouched position facing east, aligned roughly along the main axis of the cave. Although the pottery sherds from Bur Mghez belong to the Gġantija and Tarxien phases of

Mġarr Temple

It is thought by Professor John Evans that the basic ground plan of the temples owes its origin to that of the underground architecture of the rock-cut Zebbug Phase tombs. (As we shall see below, this process was to be reversed at a future date when features of the above ground temple architecture were incorporated into the subterranean Hal Saflieni Hypogeum complex). It is also possible that there might have been some less durable above ground precursor for the temples that has not survived.

The first three of the five stages of development of the ground plan of the temples belong to this phase. The first stage consisted of a lobed or kidney-shaped plan as exemplified by Mġarr (Malta) East.
The addition of an apse to the kidney shape marked the trefoil or three-apsed second stage (as at Kordin,

Skorba Temple.

Skorba and elsewhere), and the further addition of an extra kidney shape constitutes the third stage five-apsed plan as can be seen at Ġgantija South and Tarxien East.

From modest beginnings the temples spread all over the islands and assumed monumental proportions, dominating the skyline, much as their present day equivalents do.

They were probably three times higher than their current ruins stand. One of the most impressive of these monuments is Ġgantija in Gozo, the type site for this phase. Built of gargantuan megaliths, each several tons in weight, our forebears were convinced that it could only have been erected by a race of giants, hence its name.

It is not certain how, or if, these temples were roofed; no trace of a ceiling survives. However, in places the successive courses of stone draw inwards as they go up, narrowing the aperture at the top, so this method of corbelling of the stone courses suggests an attempt at roofing the aperture.

This could have been accomplished by further courses of stone, which were then capped with ceiling slabs. Alternatively, the aperture at the top could have been covered with timber, animal hides and plaster. The evidence from a contemporary small stone model and scratched depictions of a temple that survive does suggest that these buildings were roofed. Traces of plaster and red pigment show that the inner walls were smooth and painted.

The Maltese temples are a local indigenous development reflecting the peculiar culture and beliefs of this insular people. Although there is nothing quite like them anywhere else, they should not however be divorced from the general context of European megalithic culture. Some of the most intriguing questions in Maltese archaeology are associated with these buildings. How and why were they built, what was their purpose, and what led to their eventual decline?

The heavy concentration of these magnificent monuments in such small islands is remarkable. At least twenty-three of these temples are known to have existed in the Maltese Islands. Their large size indicates that they could not have

Tarxien Temple - Showing Corbelling.

been the work of small local families, and that a fair degree of social organisation was involved in mobilising a labour force sufficient for their erection. It is estimated that the population of the Islands could have been around 11,000, and it is suggested that they were divided into five or six groups or territories, each numbering about 2,000. Each territory contains a cluster of two or more temples and is headed by a chief who commands a major area of the arable land available on the Islands. Under this proposed chiefdom system with a central organisation, works on the scale of the temples could be undertaken. The temples served not only a social religious function, but also an economic one where the distribution of gifts to and by the chief, in the form of produce, could take place, allowing the development of specialisation of crafts, including that of a priestly class, potters, fishermen, construction workers and the like.

This chiefdom society proposed by Lord Renfrew seems the explanation most likely to account for the presence of this concentration of magnificent monuments in such an unlikely environment.

Parochial rivalry could also have spurred one group, as it does to this day, to outshine the rival groups in the splendour of their edifice. These buildings were erected without the aid of metal tools or the wheel. Ropes were probably used to haul the megaliths into position, and round stones the size of a football placed beneath the megaliths helped in their manoeuvering.

The discovery of a colossal statue, statuettes and figurines of the "Maltese Fat Lady" in the temples, together with the presence of animal offerings in niches and behind altars, suggests a cult of the

Tarxien Temple complex.

Spiral Relief (Tarxien).

"Mother Goddess of Fertility", even though most of the statues appear to be of indeterminate sex. A number of phallic statuettes has also been uncovered, showing Neolithic man's recognition of this organ's reproductive powers.

The temples were the seat of authority, both economic and religious. Indentations in stones near the entrances appear to be supports for door hinges and securing poles. Other connecting holes on the exterior stones appear to have been used for the tethering of animals.

Whilst the priests conducted their magico-religious ritual within the temple's apses, the people and their animals gathered in the outside forecourt.

Other holes are thought to have served the oracle, where an often ambiguous or obscure response was provided to a question, or perhaps a dream might be interpreted.

It has also been pointed out that most of the temples share a similar north-west south-east alignment, and it is claimed that an astronomical calendar is carved into one of the blocks of the Mnajdra complex. Among the more imaginative suggestions is that the temples could also have served some sacred prostitution function, and the five-apsed Temple plan has also been likened to the shape of the "Mother Goddess", the main entrance representing her vagina.

The staple diet of these temple people was barley and wheat, and

Seated "Mother Goddess" statuette.

IV) SAFLIENI PHASE
(3,000 - 2,900 B.C.)

This is a short transitional phase during which some new pottery shapes and types of decoration occur, typified by the biconical "Saflieni" bowl.

they reared sheep, goats, cattle and pigs as well as harvesting produce from the sea. The potters of the Ġgantija Phase were more adventurous than their predecessors, introducing several new shapes, and characteristically decorating the pots by scratching lines on the surface after firing, and sometimes covering these with a red ochre paste.

"Mother Goddess" statuette.

Stone Temple Altar from Ħaġar Qim.

ĦAĠAR QIM

V) TARXIEN PHASE
(3,000 - 2,500 B.C.)

Procession of animals (Tarxien).

This phase marks the acme of the Temple civilisation, as well as its sudden decline and mysterious disappearance at the end. It sees the last two stages in the development of the temple plan. The penultimate stage sees the replacement of the far apse by a shallow altar niche (as in sections of the Tarxien, Hagar Qim and Mnajdra complexes), and the final stage of three symmetrical pairs of apses finds expression only in the central unit at Tarxien.

The temples of this last phase are the most refined of the temple culture, both technically and aesthetically. Not only are the megaliths neater and better dressed than before, but some are also adorned with relief sculpture. Variations on the theme of the

Mnajdra Temple.

spiral are the commonest, and there are also processions of different species of animal. In the seaside temple at Buġibba relief carving depicting fish was found. An enormous seated "Mother Goddess" statue, over 2 metres in height, stood in the vestibule of the Tarxien temple complex. The original stone sculptures are preserved in the National Museum of Archaeology, and copies have been placed on site.

Pottery craftsmanship also reached its summit during this phase of the temple culture, and, like the monuments, the shapes and decoration seem to be of an indigenous character. Most shapes are angular with little in the way of handles, and a scratched volute decoration is the most popular. The foundations of a primitive dwelling hut of the Temple Period were discovered in Ghajnsielem, Gozo in the late 1980's, and, added to the traces of a few others at

Skorba in Malta, that is about the sum of the domestic architecture that has come to light from this period. The wide gulf in splendour between religious and domestic architecture that existed in the Temple Period has narrowed in recent times.

Mnajdra Temple.

THE HYPOGEUM AND BROCHTORFF CIRCLE

The dawn of the temple civilisation marked the first burials in Malta with the appearance of the Zebbug Phase rock-cut family graves. We do not know how man disposed of his dead before this period. Coinciding with the emergence of the temples in the Ġgantija Phase, which necessitated a substantial degree of social organisation, there came about a revolution in mortuary practice. The individual and the family were no longer so important and the emphasis now shifts to the community at large; a sort of megalithic communism. Imposing communal burial grounds now replace the individual family tombs. The temple builders of Malta are buried in the Hal-Saflieni Hypogeum, which is close to the Tarxien Temples, whereas those in Gozo find their final resting place in the Xaghra (Brochtorff) Stone Circle, adjacent to the Ġgantija Temples. And there may well have been three or four other communal burial grounds that we are unaware of, serving the other districts.

The Hypogeum, a UNESCO World Heritage Site, as are the Temples, is a unique three-storey multi-chambered underground rock-cut structure hewn out without the aid of metal tools. Although primarily a burial site it also appears to have served other ritual functions. The bones of an estimated number of 7,000 individuals were discovered in its chambers in the early part of the 20th century, along with personal ornaments, pottery, and figurines which include that icon of the Maltese patrimony, the so called "Sleeping Lady". There are also rock-cut architectural features which faithfully imitate structures found in the above ground temples, such as trilithons, blind niche "altar" structures as well as corbelling of the walls. This reverses the process whereby it is thought that the underground rock-cut tombs of the Zebbug Phase provided inspiration for the first above ground temple ground plan. Intricate spiral designs in red ochre are also found on the walls in the Hypogeum, such as in the "Holy of Holies".

Hypogeum - Rock cut features imitating temple structures.

The Xaghra Brochtorff Stone Circle, rediscovered in the 1960's and excavated in the late 1980's-1990's, also yielded the bones of several thousand individuals, and is the Gozitan equivalent in function of the Hypogeum in Malta. It differs somewhat in structure, however, as the essential units comprising this complex are composed of a warren of natural subterranean caves and cavities, albeit with some modifications. A section of this site was left undisturbed for future generations of archaeologists to ponder on.

Funerary ritual, (which appears to have been by primary inhumation in family tombs in the Zebbug Phase), changed with the utilisation of these two sites. Not only were one's ancestors no longer deposited in the family tomb where they could be selectively venerated, but the rite of secondary deposition was introduced. Most of the bones recovered from these two sites were disarticulated, indicating transport subsequent to the defleshing of the body. A ritual including the interference with defleshed bones is confirmed by the vast number of bones rubbed with red ochre discovered at Xaghra; this could only have occurred post decomposition. A few articulated individuals were discovered, including a youngster with a puppy, but most of the bones were anatomically sorted into groups; skulls with skulls, femora with femora and the like.

The entrances to the natural cavities in the Brochtorff Circle were given greater formality by the addition of megalithic blocks, and the whole site was enclosed by a megalithic circle of some 120 metres in circumference. Among the artefacts excavated from this site are two "firsts" for Maltese prehistoric figurative art. These are the cache of nine stylised limestone figurines dubbed "Shaman's Sticks" and a statuette representing a 'twin' pair of seated "Mother Goddesses", one holding a baby replica and the other some

form of vessel.
The proximity of these large communal cemeteries to the impressive temple complexes of Tarxien and Ġgantija respectively could indicate a ritual connection with a possible processional route between the sites. We do not know precisely where or how the bodies were defleshed, but it seems to have been a natural process as no cut marks on the bones have come to light. They could either have been interred in the earth and dug up after decomposition for

secondary burial, or, alternatively, excarnation could have been accomplished by exposure in the open air.

The unique island civilisation that was Malta's temple culture reached its climax in the Tarxien Phase. The people were essentially neolithic farmers but with a degree of social organisation that permitted the construction of the earliest free-standing monuments of stone in the world (dating from about 3,600 B.C.), and that directed the burial of

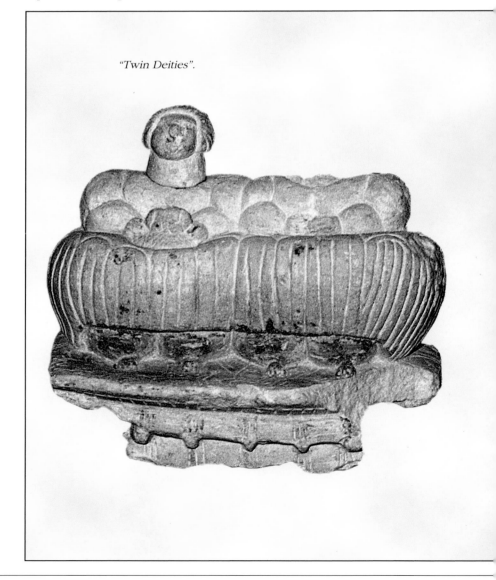

"Twin Deities".

the dead into large communal centralised cemeteries that were utilised for over a millennium. They appear to have been generally healthy and well fed, and to have enjoyed a peaceful existence. No evidence of weapons of war, military fortifications or battle trauma to the skeletons has emerged from this period.

Although these people appear to have been of the same average stature as their current Maltese counterparts, some skulls surviving at the Hypogeum are a little narrower and longer. They had a markedly lower incidence of dental caries than is inflicted on the present population; sugar had not yet been discovered.

The statues show that they had tailored clothing of woven fabric, and their hair was cut and styled with braids.

They wore bead and shell necklaces, and had divans of carefully woven reeds or cane.

Hagar Qim.

What brought this civilisation to an end in approximately 2,500 B.C. remains one of the most elusive mysteries of Maltese prehistory. It could well be, however, that climatic changes affected the agricultural economic base precipitating its demise.

A glorious era of Maltese prehistory with splendid accomplishments in architecture and sculpture was over.

The people and culture that were to follow were of an entirely different nature.

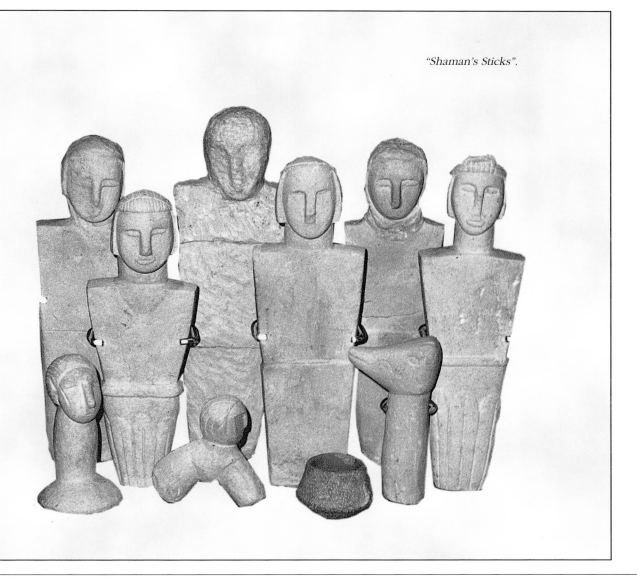

"Shaman's Sticks".

5. THE BRONZE AGE (2,500 - 700 B.C.)

I) TARXIEN CEMETERY PHASE (2,500 - 1,500 B.C.)

It is not known quite where this new group appeared from, but they had features in common with other Bronze Age warriors occupying the central Mediterranean at that time.

They differed from their temple period predecessors in their material and social culture. They introduced metal into Malta for the first time, in the shape of bronze and copper tools and weapons, and another first for Malta was the manner in which these people disposed of their dead; it was they who introduced cremation to the Islands.

Indeed the type site that represents this phase is the Tarxien cremation cemetery, excavated by Sir Themistocles Zammit, the grand old man of Maltese archaeology. It was located in a dark grey ashy layer above the layer of "abandonment" right in the middle of the Tarxien temple complex. This is a good example of the reutilisation of a sacred place by different people at different times, albeit, in this case, for a different purpose.

If the old temples had wooden roofing beams these could have been used for the funeral pyres, though it is not certain that cremation took place on the site. About one hundred crushed cinerary urns, some one metre high, contained incompletely cremated human bones as well as various personal ornaments and other objects, the latter not having been subjected to cremation. These included pottery vessels of various shapes and sizes, figurines, pendants, beads and copper tools and weapons. Clumps of charred textile of a yellow reddish colour show that the bodies were cremated in a dyed woven flax shroud. Silver objects were also found, this being the first recorded example of this metal in Malta, and carbonised barley seeds indicate an agricultural offering. The pottery consists mostly of jugs and bowls, often decorated with incised geometric patterns, and sometimes joined together in groups of two or three. It bears some resemblance to the pottery of the Capo Graziano culture of Lipari.

Dolmen.

Although in possession of the advanced technology of metallurgy, there seems little else to indicate any superiority of this new group over their temple period predecessors. No trace of where or how these people lived has yet come to light. Practically the only architectural feature associated with this one thousand year phase is the DOLMEN, several examples of which survive scattered throughout the Islands. The dolmen consists of a huge horizontal irregular block of stone supported on three sides by blocks of smaller stone. Although there is no proof, it is thought that these dolmens served a funerary function, probably as a repository for cinerary urns.

There are also a number of solitary standing megaliths distributed around the Islands known as MENHIRS. Although they have been associated with this Phase, there is evidence that some of them, at least, are simply the last remaining stones of some Temple period structure.

II) Borg in-Nadur Phase
(1,500 - 725 B.C.)

Mounting insecurity in the Mediterranean is evidenced in Malta by the second Bronze Age phase, the type site of which is the fortified village of Borg in-Nadur, located on a promontory above the southern Maltese harbour of Marsaxlokk. The need for defence was clearly felt and this was provided by the natural steep sides of the promontory.

To fortify its flatter landward side a massive rampart of cyclopean stones was erected to complete the defences. Promontories or high flat-topped defensible hills are the typical sites of this Bronze Age phase, and one such is the hilltop of Nuffara in Gozo, where another typical feature of this phase can be found. This consists of shallow rock-hewn globular or bell-shaped pits thought to have been used for storage of water and grain.

Examples of these "silo pits" can

also be seen in the rocks at the water's edge in Marsaxlokk below the Borg in-Nadur site where grain might have been stored for export. Some of the pits are now submerged, testimony to the alteration in land/sea levels since those times. Cart ruts also disappear into the sea at this site. Borg in-Nadur also provides evidence for the working of metal, and of the pottery characteristic of the phase, which has a flaky red surface slip and zigzag incised decoration with a white paste inlay. The dwellings in the village at Borg in-Nadur consisted of oval huts on stone foundations.

III) Bahrija Phase
(900 - 700 B.C.)

The last two centuries of the Bronze Age sees the appearance of a new group who seem to have intermingled with the indigenous population. Their characteristic dark pottery suggests an origin from Calabria in Southern Italy, and the type site of this group is the settlement on a promontory at Bahrija known as Qlejgha.

Menhir.

More numerous in Malta than in Gozo, the cart ruts represent the most enigmatic feature of the local archaeological patrimony. It is not even certain to what period they belong, so they are dealt with here as a separate entity, straddling the prehistoric and historic periods. The fact that some tracks disappear over cliff edges (due to subsequent collapse) and others vanish into the sea (due to altered land/sea levels), is testimony of their great antiquity.

Traditionally assigned to the Bronze Age, and even to the Temple period, there are some who now argue for a more recent origin. One of the proofs in support of a prehistoric origin is the contention that a pair of cart ruts are intersected and cut into by a more recent Punic tomb of the historic period. However, on examination of the site at Mtarfa I could not confirm this assertion. A pair of cart

tracks does indeed lead up to the entrance of a Punic tomb, but there is no evidence of them emerging at the far side, where the hard coralline limestone is on a slightly higher level and would surely have preserved the tracks had they been present. This does not prove anything but it leaves the question open.

Professor Anthony Bonanno has

noted that the Maltese cart ruts tend to occur in close association with stone quarries of the historic Phoenician and Roman periods, and therefore suggests that they could well belong to this chronological period.

Their purpose appears to be connected with some form of transport system and it seems that they were intentionally cut into the rock and are not simply the result of wear from some sort of vehicle. What manner of vehicle used them is also open to question though wheeled carts and slide carts on stone runners are the likely contenders.

We are also not sure how these vehicles were propelled. There is no evidence of any track worn out either between the ruts or to their sides that could have been caused by man or beast.

THE HISTORICAL PERIOD

6. ANTIQUITY

I) THE PHOENICIANS
(APPROX. 725 - 218 B.C.)

Phoenician Pottery

The people whom we call the Phoenicians are the descendants of the biblical Canaanites. This great seafaring and trading people are credited with being the inventors of the alphabet, and the arrival of these literate people in Malta in the early half of the eighth century B.C. represents a watershed in the story of these Islands. Writing was introduced and Malta entered the Historic Period.

Early traces of this ancient Phoenician colony are found at the Tas-Silg sanctuary overlooking Marsaxlokk harbour on the south-east coast of Malta. Phoenician pottery is intermingled with that of the resident Borg in-Nadur phase Bronze Age population and it seems that the establishment of the colony was undertaken in a relatively peaceful manner. They brought with them their gods from the Levant, and the sanctuary they established at Tas-Silg was dedicated to Astarte. Later, under Punic influence, she was to become known as Tanit.

Phoenician settlements were also established inland in the neighbourhood of Rabat Malta, and Rabat Gozo, probably also Bronze Age sites, and these two citadel sites would eventually become the main town centres in Roman times. Early Phoenician tombs from this period not only contain the typical Levantine funerary pottery assembly but also Greek and Rhodian imports datable to the early 8th and late 7th centuries B.C. Malta was one of the key points on the trading route between the Levant in the east and the western Mediterranean Phoenician colonies.

Changing political circumstances in the Levant, with pressure coming from the Assyrian and Neo-Babylonian empires, diminished the power of the Phoenician mother city states there, and the Maltese Islands, after a couple of centuries or so, were to fall more into the ambit of that great Phoenician colony in North Africa which became known as Punic Carthage. The Phoenician period of Malta is therefore more properly called the Phoenicio-Punic period.

National Museum of Archaeology.

Moreover the cultural influence of this period long outlived its historical chronological confines. Although the Romans conquered Malta in 218 B.C. Punic cultural influence extended well into the first century A.D. (and beyond) as is attested by the discovery of a Neo-Punic inscription of that date in a catacomb in Rabat. Mere political change is not sufficient to stamp out immediately centuries old cultural traditions.

And what tradition is more fundamental and resistant to change than that of the burial ritual? A change of burial ritual indicates a cultural change of the utmost import. It may represent the presence of an entirely new people, as when cremation was introduced in the Bronze Age. It could also represent the appearance of a new religion amongst a stable population, as when the Christian rite of inhumation replaced the pagan Roman and Punic practice of cremation at a later date. The use of Punic rock-cut tombs all over the Maltese Islands extended well into the Roman period, showing that Roman occupation did little to affect the burial traditions of the Maltese.

On the other hand the strategic maritime central Mediterranean position of the Islands exposed them to a wide range of cultural influences. Both before, during and after the Roman political and military hegemony, Malta did not escape the changes brought about by the Mediterranean spread of the ubiquitous Greek Hellenistic culture. It is for this reason that a broad non-political cultural term is often used to denote much of the Phoenician/Roman episode in Maltese history, namely the Punico-Hellenistic period.

It was this cultural mix that produced the two large hardstone *candelabrae* discovered in Malta, datable to the 2nd century B.C. They are set upon a plinth inscribed bilingually in Punic and Greek, bearing a dedication to the Punic god Melqart and his Greek equivalent Herakles. These important inscriptions proved instrumental in deciphering the Phoenician language - much as the Rosetta Stone paved the way for our understanding of Egyptian hieroglyphics. One of these

Tas-Silg Sanctuary, a multi-period site.

candelabrae can be viewed at the National Museum of Archaeology in Valletta whilst its companion is in the Louvre in Paris.

Punic culture was also influenced by the Egyptians, and this is evidenced in the impressive remains of a "Phoenician" building in Zurrieq which is crowned by a gorge cornice of Egyptian inspiration. Other Egyptianising influences on Punic Maltese culture can be seen in the amulets recovered from Punic tombs.

Having settled peacefully on the Islands the Phoenicians established settlements often in close proximity to the hilltop sites of their Bronze Age predecessors; indeed there may even have been a period of cohabitation. They also re-utilised the late Temple Period Sanctuary at Tas-Silg, modifying the Tarxien phase temple to their exigencies. Later it was to become the Roman temple of Juno, plundered by Caius Verres of two magnificent ivory tusks. Tas-Silg is an important multi-period site extensively excavated a few decades ago and currently undergoing further investigation.

As the population prospered and grew throughout the Phoenicio-Punic period, imbibing outside cultural influences as a result of their trading activities, the Maltese landscape became peppered with urban, rural and harbour settlements. The location patterning and size of the widespread Punic rock-cut cemeteries gives us a good indication of Phoenician settlement pattern in Malta. Burial, incidentally, was both by inhumation and cremation, both rites often being encountered in the same tomb. There is no evidence for the Phoenician practice of child sacrifice in Malta; no tophets have been found. Neither do claims that the Phoenician language gave origin to the present day Maltese tongue hold any water. The Maltese language derives from a much more recent semitic occupation.

An inscription on a late Punic bronze coin gives the name for Malta as ANAN, though the ancient name in common use was MELITE. This could either derive from the Semitic word for refuge or harbour, or from the Greek and Latin word for honey, both denotations having associations with the island.

Other than the normal Phoenician-type red slipped burnished pottery, a host of other artefacts has been recovered from the numerous rock-

Bilingual Candelabrum
(National Museum of Archaeology).

cut shaft and chamber tombs. These include various items of gold and silver: bangles, earrings, beads, rings, a pair of amulets and thin foil. The amulets most commonly encountered are of Egyptian gods in faience, though one interesting 6th century B.C. amulet of Horus is in bronze, and contains a papyrus carrying a Phoenician inscription in five lines with the image of the goddess Isis. The text exhorts the deceased to overcome his enemies in the netherworld. Numerous scarab rings with magical hieroglyphic texts invoking the protection of Egyptian gods have also been found in Punic tombs in Rabat, as has a bronze torch holder.

The rise of Rome and her challenge of Carthage for supremacy in the central Mediterranean gave birth to the Punic Wars. During the first of these wars, probably in 253 B.C., Malta was ravaged by a Roman attack under the command of Attilius Regulus. The Carthaginians

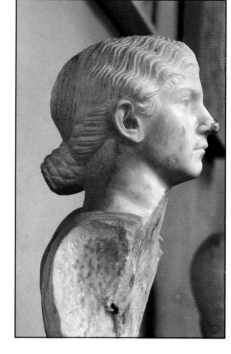

Roman Statuary.

held on to Malta, but their grip on the Islands was coming to an end.

II) THE ROMANS
(218 B.C. - 535 A.D.)

The conflict between Rome and Carthage for domination of the central Mediterranean led to Malta being incorporated within the Roman commonwealth in 218 B.C. The Roman historian Titus Livius records that on that date (by extrapolation of course) the Roman Consul Tiberius Sempronius Longus set sail from Lilybaeum (Marsala) in Sicily in search of the Carthaginian fleet. This was the start of the Hannibalic or Second Punic War. The local garrison of just under 2,000 troops under the command of the Carthaginian general Hamilcar surrendered to the Romans, and Malta became part of the newly conquered Roman province of Sicily.

The Maltese Islands had had close contact with Sicily since earliest times. The first man in Malta had crossed over from Sicily. But henceforth, till the coming of the Knights Hospitiller in 1530, the two Islands were to share a much closer destiny. We know that in the first centuries of Roman rule Malta was governed internally by a senate and a people's assembly, with Gozo having some form of administrative autonomy. In Republican times both islands were centrally governed by the propraetor of Sicily; Caius Verres, in the years 73 - 71 B.C., being a notorious example. Under the Empire it appears that Malta had a procurator directly responsible to the Emperor in Rome. We also know from several inscriptions that have survived, that under the Empire, (2nd Century A.D.), both Malta and Gozo enjoyed municipal status.

Probably the most significant event recorded during the Roman occupation was the shipwreck of Saints Paul and Luke on the Islands in A.D. 60. There are some who have disputed this fact and lay counter-claims for an island of the Dalmatian coast as the site of the shipwreck. But the overwhelming thrust of the evidence seems to point to Malta as the likely site.

This episode has spawned much local tradition concerning St. Paul, and he is deeply revered in Malta as its patron saint. Tradition tells us that St. Paul converted the whole of the Maltese population to Christianity, and that they have remained Christian uninterruptedly ever since. There are also many less credible traditions associated with the Saints' three months sojourn on the Island.

As regards the first mentioned tradition it is interesting to note that St. Luke's account of the shipwreck in the New Testament makes no mention of any conversion of the Maltese. Neither is there any archaeological evidence to support such a contention. The first such undisputed testimony to the practice of the Christian religion in the Maltese Islands dates to the first part of the 4th century A.D., and this evidence derives from the catacombs.

The Acts of the Apostles, chapter 28, referring to the Saints' shipwreck on the Islands, tells us

San Pawl Milqghi.

that the chief man of Malta was called Publius, and that Paul healed his father of a fever and bloody flux, as well as curing other sick islanders. No mention is made of Publius being converted, still less of his being created the first Bishop of Malta, as tradition has it. The islanders were so impressed at Paul's immunity to a venomous viper that they thought he was a god. Presumably, some were converted; if not openly at least covertly. More about the other traditions below.

It is also interesting to note in St. Luke's account that he refers to the Maltese as "barbarians"; in other words they spoke a language that was neither Greek nor Latin. Presumably the Punic language had survived some three centuries or so of Roman occupation.

Some information on life in Roman Malta is provided by the Latin orator Cicero (1st century B.C.), who informs us of the high quality of the local textile industry, of the practice of pirates sheltering for the winter in Maltese harbours, and of the international veneration accorded to the local temple dedicated to the god Juno. He also mentions a fine collection of silverware in the house of a resident of Malta.

Diodorus Siculus, another writer of the same period, informs us that "the dwellings on the Island are worthy of note, being ambitiously constructed". Ptolemy (2nd century A.D.) tells us that there was a main town on each of the islands, Melite in Malta and Gaulos (or Gaudos) in Gozo. There are also numerous

allusions in classical literature to Maltese dogs; they are mentioned at least twice in Aesop's fables.

For the most part, however, we must rely on archaeological evidence to inform us of life in Roman Malta.

The Roman town of Melite comprised present day Mdina and much of Rabat, as far as the ditch behind St. Paul's church, beyond which the extensive Roman tombs are found. Within the town stood a temple dedicated to Apollo and other official buildings. The most impressive archaeological remains from Roman Malta must surely be the town house in Melite which today is known as the 'Museum of Roman Antiquities' in Rabat. This splendid and stately house dates to the 1st century B.C. and contains a large peristyle in the Doric order plastered in coloured stucco. Much of the house is embellished with mosaics of the finest quality, and it also contains groups of imperial portrait statues as well as a host of other artefacts. It could well be one of the dwellings referred to by Diodorus Siculus.

Whilst urban life was concentrated

in the two main towns of the Islands, the countryside was scattered with villas or country estates of which we have knowledge of more than thirty. Most of these had extensive outbuildings and were equipped for agricultural purposes. Apparatus for the processing of olive oil has often been found in these villas and the countryside must have been resplendent with a verdant olive aspect. A well preserved villa of this type can be visited at San Pawl Milqghi.

Museum of Roman antiquities, mosaic.

Other villas appear to have been
more of a country retreat residential
type such as that at Għajn Tuffieħa,
equipped with mosaiced thermal
baths and communal latrine, and
the one situated in Ramla Bay Gozo
which has a heated bathing system
and marble floors.

There were also coastal fishing
settlements and harbour facilities,
the most significant remains of
which have been found in the inner
Marsa area of the Grand Harbour.
Salina Bay has also turned up a
number of Roman lead anchors and
innumerable amphorae, as has
Xlendi Bay in Gozo.

Although relatively little remains of
above ground Roman structures,
Malta is rich in Roman burial sites.
Their distribution pattern
throughout the Islands and their
concentration gives a good
indication as to the population
density of the time. The major
concentration of tombs occurs in
the Rabat area beyond the walls of
the old town of Melite, and smaller

clusters of tombs are scattered throughout the Islands, serving the outlying communities.

The first few centuries of Roman rule did little to affect the burial customs of the native Maltese Punic stock. Burial was in a rock-cut tomb served by a shaft leading to one or two funerary chambers. It was not before the 1st century A.D. that miniature catacombs began to be developed, though the basic chambered shaft-tomb remained in vogue, particularly in the country districts, throughout the late Roman and even Byzantine periods. The tombs were sealed with bulky stone plugs, sealing slabs, and even large monolithic pivotal doors on occasion in the later more elaborate catacombs.

Though not as large as the Italian catacombs, those in Malta are rich in architectural detail and contain some unique features. Eight different types of tomb have been identified within the catacombs, of which the commonly occurring

Funerary Triclinium.

The Catacombs.

window-tomb appears to be peculiar to Malta. What is also characteristic of the Maltese catacombs is the Funerary Triclinium or Agape Table often encountered in some prominent position. It is a low cylindrical table with sloping sides for reclining on, the whole being hewn out of the rock to form a single architectural unit. They seem to have served the purpose of holding refrigeria, or commemorative meals, near the tombs on death anniversaries. This originally pagan practice was taken up by the Christians though a strict prohibition against it was issued by the Council of Trullo in 692 A.D.

The Rabat area contains Pagan, Jewish and Christian catacombs. These are distinguished not by their architecture or their siting, for they are intermingled, but by their decoration and contents. Thus a Jewish tomb is indicated by an incised Menorah or seven-branched candlestick, and the cross or cross monogram indicates a Christian burial. The decoration on the pottery oil lamps, the nature of an inscription or the iconography of a mural also help in identifying the religious persuasion of the deceased. There is no secure evidence for any Christian burial before the early 4th century A.D.

when Constantine made his peace with the Church and Christianity was allowed to flourish in the Empire.

Throughout the Roman period Malta was a minor provincial outpost that played no significant role in political or military affairs.

The Catacombs.

There are, however, the remains of a group of round towers in Malta, principally on the South of the island, whose purpose appears to have been defensive. Variously assigned to prehistoric or Phoenician times, they are now thought to be Roman, and the one at Ta' Gawhar appears to have been destroyed towards the end of the third century A.D.

Whilst the official government, religion and language was Roman, as we know from several surviving inscriptions, the underlying culture remained Punico-Hellenistic, and at some time in the early 4th century A.D. became openly Christian.

With the decline of Empire Malta became subject to the vicissitudes of the time. It may be inferred from

a reference of Victor Bishop of Vita in North Africa, writing at the end of the 5th century A.D., that the Islands were conquered by the Vandals of North Africa, (as was Sicily), from about 455 to 476 A.D. The likelihood is that Malta was then granted to Odoacer, the barbarian king of Italy, in return for tribute, and around 495 A.D. passed to the hands of Theodoric, the Ostrogothic king, after his defeat of Odoacer. There is no archaeological evidence of any incursion or change of regime in this poorly documented period which marks the end of Rome's rule in Malta.

III) THE BYZANTINES
(535 - 780 A.D.)

Astride late antiquity and the early medieval period Malta passed into Byzantine hands, under control from Constantinople, in the first half of the 6th century A.D., at around the same time as the Byzantine conquest of Sicily in 535 A.D. Procopius, in his Bellum Vandalicum, tells us that the great Byzantine General Belisarius "touched" at Malta and Gozo for a day in 533 A.D., but it seems that the Islands were still under Ostrogothic rule at the time.

Byzantine domination confirmed the pre-eminence of Christianity in Malta, and it is now that the first secure evidence of a Bishop of Malta emerges. After an ambiguous mention in 553 A.D., the first

unequivocal references to a bishop in Malta come in the register of letters of Pope Gregory the Great. The Pope writes to the Bishop Lucillus in 592 A.D., and in 598 A.D. he writes to the Bishop of Syracuse ordering him to depose Lucillus for some misdemeanour. A third letter of 599 A.D., addressed to Romanus *defensor Siciliae,* orders him to urge Lucillus and his son to hand over the property they had taken from the Church to the new bishop Traianus.

The Catacombs.

Other scant documentary evidence concerning Malta during this period shows that the Islands were used as a place of exile for rebels. In 637 A.D. Theodorus, nephew of Emperor Heraclius, had his nose and hands cut off, and was sent to the island called 'Gaudomelete' where the 'dux' was ordered to amputate one of his feet on arrival.

Byzantine rule brought an increased influence of Hellenic culture to Malta, and it is known that there was a significant influx of Greek-speaking settlers into the central Mediterranean at this time. Greek seems to have been the official language, and it probably gained importance also as a *lingua franca*.

Something of the military and civil administration of the islands can be inferred from an 8th century seal which carries the name of Nicetas, a *droungarios* and *archon* of Malta. It has been deduced from this that Malta was governed by a high ranking naval official who commanded a small fleet. With the spread of Islam across North Africa these were certainly troubled times for the Byzantine Empire, and although raids in this area began in the 7th century, the fact that Malta

did not fall into Muslim hands until 870 suggests that the Islands were reasonably well defended.

The major archaeological remains from this time are indubitably the many Christian tombs and catacombs, some of which suggest an influence from the *ecclesia africana*. An inscription in Greek from a tomb dated to the 6th century A.D. reads: "Here lies Domesticus the kindly Christian and Doctor. He lived 73 years.......". This is the second recorded man of medicine in Malta, the first being St. Luke. (Apart from being a physician St. Luke also had something of a reputation as an artist, though scrutiny of paintings reputedly executed by him in Malta lends no support to their having such a provenance). Some interesting tombs from the late Roman/Byzantine period suggest that they were reserved for members of particular professions, a sort of burial club. Thus tomb sealing slabs are found on which are carved the instruments for metal workers, stone masons, farmers and

the medical profession. There is also evidence of a Byzantine basilica at Tas-Silg, the fourth in line of sacred buildings on this site, all from a different period, and representing different faiths. It appears to have been destroyed at around the time of the Arab conquest.

The Catacombs.

7. MEDIEVAL

I) THE ARABS (870 - 1091 A.D.)

The Aghlabid Muslim rulers of Tunisia captured Palermo in 831 A.D., but it was not before 878 A.D. that most of Sicily came under their control. An attempt to take Malta was made in 869 A.D., but it was not until the following year that the definitive Muslim conquest by the Aghlabid governor of Sicily succeeded. This event is a landmark in Maltese history.

Stern reprisals were taken against the Maltese Christians. An inscription on a castle at Sousse, Tunisia, recorded that "All the hewn stones and marble columns in this castle were brought here from the conquest of Malta". Archaeological evidence from the Maltese sites of San Pawl Milqghi and Tas-Silg shows signs of destruction at levels corresponding to the arrival of the Arabs. We also know that the Bishop of Malta was to be found in chains at Palermo in 878 A.D., and that no subsequent Bishop of Malta is mentioned until 1156 A.D.

The Arab chronicler Al-Himyari records (translated in J. M. Brincat): "They captured the fortress of Malta and took its ruler Amros prisoner and they demolished its fortress, and they looted and desecrated whatever they could not carry. And he took to Ahmad from the churches of Malta that with which he built his castle in Sousse............After that, the island of Malta remained an uninhabited ruin but it was visited by shipbuilders, because the wood in it is of the strongest kind, by fishermen, because of the abundance and tastiness of the fish around its shores, and by those who collect honey, because that is the most common thing there".

"After the year 440 A.H. (i.e. some 185 years after the conquest), the Muslims peopled it and they built its city, and then it became a finer place than it was before".

The fate of Christianity in Malta under Arab rule is one of the intriguing questions of Maltese history. It seems that the population was decimated and the island an uninhabited ruin for much of the period of Muslim rule, though it is possible that a few survivors of the 870 A.D. conquest may have eked out a troglodytic existence. There is no archaeological evidence of the practice of Christianity in the period of Muslim rule in Malta.

In about 1040/1054 A.D. (the date is elusive) the Islands were repopulated by the Muslims, but within a few years there ensued an attempt by the Byzantines to retake Malta. They were bloodily repulsed by the Muslims and their slaves (who outnumbered their masters), and in recognition of their assistance the slaves were given their freedom. It is not before the coming of Count Roger the Norman in 1091 that any reference is made to Christians in Arab Malta; and these were slaves.

Practically the only archaeological remains from the Arab period are tombs, and these are all Muslim. Indeed most of them postdate the Christian attack on the Islands in 1091, showing the persisting influence for a while of Islam in Malta. There seems little doubt that Islam was the majority religion of Muslim Malta. However, claims for the existence of a mosque at Tas-Silg appear difficult to substantiate. If confirmed, it would represent the fifth in line of religious buildings on this site. There must have been a mosque at Mdina, though no trace of it has yet been discovered. It may well have been destroyed by subsequent Christian zeal.

Arab Tombstone - Museum of Roman Antiquities, Rabat.

There is no doubt that the most enduring legacy of Arab occupation is in the language, surnames and place names of the Island. Other than in the genes they sowed. The Maltese language is derived from Arabic, the kind of Tunisian Arabic spoken in eleventh century Sicily. Being a living language Maltese has of course taken on innumerable loan words since then. Principally Italian, some French, and many English words have been added on to the underlying Siculo-Arabic substrate. Politically motivated claims that the Maltese language derives from the Phoenician, or is a Romance language, remain just that. The first recorded instance of Maltese being used as a written language is Pietru Caxaru's "Kantilena" of the mid-1400's.

It must be said, however, that our knowledge of the period of Arab rule in Malta is somewhat sketchy. Although the Arab chroniclers record that Malta remained an uninhabited ruin for much of this time, recent archaeological investigations in Mdina (so named by the Arabs) and elsewhere seem to throw a different light on the period. Nathaniel Cutajar has discovered the presence in abundance of imported Islamic ceramic ware from both North Africa and Sicily, showing that Mdina was occupied throughout the 11th century, and probably in the late 10th century as well. Malta appears to have been participating in the trade engendered by Arab rule in the Maghreb and Sicily at that time.

Much remains to be understood about this contentious period of Maltese history.

II) THE NORMANS
(1091 - 1194 A.D.)

The eleventh century A. D. saw the Normans gaining an increasing foothold in Southern Italy. Their plan for the conquest of Sicily from the Arabs had a crusade-like nature with backing from the Pope - liberating former Christian land from Muslim rule. But there were also undertones to this undertaking in outpacing the eastern Greek Byzantines in reconquest for the Latin Roman west. The conquest of Sicily was a drawn out affair which lasted some thirty years, and with the fall of Noto in 1090 plans were made for the attack on Malta.

Rather than a conquest of occupation the 1091 affair was more a razzia raid of subjugation to protect the southern defences of Sicily. The account of Count Roger the Norman's raid on Malta is given by Goffredus Malaterra, a French Benedictine in the entourage of Roger D' Hautville.

Arriving in Malta the fleet disembarked and massacred the Islanders who presented themselves to oppose Count Roger's troops. For a day he laid waste to the countryside. The following day, besieged in the city of Medina, the Arab military commander sued for peace, and the following terms were imposed on him:
1. The islanders had to submit to Count Roger and recognise him as their overlord.
2. They had to pay a yearly tribute to Count Roger.
3. They had to surrender all weapons of war.
4. All their Christian captives must be freed.

The latter poured out of the city with shouts of *"Kyrie Eleison!"*, waving palm fronds in greeting of Count Roger. The fleet returned to Sicily heavy with the burden of the freed Christian captives who were offered a town in Sicily in which to resettle. But they turned down this offer, preferring instead to return to their respective home towns.

Although he achieved the military objective of securing the southern flank of Sicily, it could be argued that Count Roger's two day raid on Malta rendered the Islands less Christian. After all, he relieved the city of all its captive Christians. And Malaterra makes no mention of any native Maltese Christian inhabitants, neither in the city nor in the countryside.

Count Roger left no known Christian garrison behind him but allowed the Muslim inhabitants to remain on the island in complete control of the administration. There is nothing to substantiate the local tradition that Count Roger built a cathedral in Mdina and numerous churches in the countryside; nor that he gave Malta its red and white national colours. The church in Mdina is first mentioned in 1299.

Significant archaeological evidence from this time is that of Muslim tombs. A large Muslim cemetery was discovered in the late 19th century which overlaid the abandoned ruins of the Roman town house in Melite referred to above. This shows that certainly by Arab times, (and probably before), the old Roman city walls had shrunk to the present position

occupied by the Mdina bastions. Some tombs had inscriptions carved on prismatic stelae, all being either verses from the Koran or Arabic personal names, all in Arabic script.

Of the ones which are dated all are post 1091, the dates ranging from 1106 to 1188, and these are preserved in an annexe of the Museum of Roman Antiquities in Rabat, where they were found. Muslim tombs have also been uncovered elsewhere on the Islands.

Life in Malta seems to have gone on pretty much as normal after Count Roger's visit, though of course there would have been some scarcity of slaves. Corsairing activity against the Byzantine rivals of the Normans may well have continued.

The definitive break in Arab rule came in 1127 when Count Roger's son King Roger reconquered the Islands on a more permanent basis than his father, and established a garrison which no doubt had Christian chaplains. The process of re-evangelisation had begun, but it was to be a slow process. Writing in 1175 Bishop Burchard of Strasbourg, in transit through Sicily, states that Malta was inhabited by Saracens; this almost fifty years after King Roger's reconquest, and confirmed by the Muslim graves in Rabat.

Palazzo Gatto Murina, Mdina.

During the first half of the twelfth century a number of poems, which have survived, were written by Maltese poets in Classical Arabic, the literary language and script. It is not known precisely when Arabic writing fell into disuse in Malta. Pietru Caxaru's fifteenth century "Kantilena" in Maltese, i.e. the demotic spoken Arabic of the Maltese people, was in Latin script, as it remains to this day.

A sizeable Muslim community was still present on the Islands in 1240 living alongside Christians and Jews. But in 1249 they were expelled by the Swabian Emperor Frederick II, who also exiled the Sicilian Muslims at the same time. It is known that the Sicilian Muslims were spared exile if they consented to being baptised, and no doubt this also applied to the Maltese Muslims, whom the present day Maltese must count amongst their forebears.

Norman rule in Malta ended in 1194 after a period of strife between King Roger's descendants and the Swabian German pretenders to the Sicilian Crown. Towards the end of Norman rule King Tancred granted the pirate Margarito of Brindisi the title of Count of Malta. This habit of alienating Malta from the royal domain by granting it to an absentee non-Maltese Count was to become commonplace in post-Norman times.

There is no trace of any Norman architecture in the Maltese Islands; the so-called "Norman House" in Mdina is from a later period. Under Norman rule ceramic ware importation from north Africa ceases, but the Islands continued to receive considerable amounts from Sicily. This is probably due to the predominance of Genoese commercial interests throughout the Tyrranean and Sicilian area, the archaeological evidence here supporting documentary history. However, Norman rule in Malta did not exhibit to the same extent the strong cultural impact it had on Sicily.

III) THE SWABIANS
(1194 - 1266 A.D.)

Henry VI was the first Swabian German ruler of Sicily, and he obtained the crown by marriage to the Norman Costanza of Sicily. Henry imprisoned Margarito and replaced him as Count of Malta with the Genoese corsair Guglielmo Grasso, who seems to have been unpopular with the Maltese, and in 1198 Costanza granted them a charter incorporating the Islands perpetually into the royal domain. This meant direct dependence on the Crown, and freedom from the Count.

However, Grasso was succeeded in 1203 by his son-in-law, the influential corsair Henry 'Pescatore', who used Malta as his base for corsairing and crusading activities. The royal charter had been rescinded.

In 1240 King Frederick II's proctor on the Island was Paolino de Malta who was entrusted with supplying the royal zoo. He sent camels and leopards to the King from Africa, and even kept camels in Malta for breeding. The King was also particularly interested in the Maltese falcons. Paolino was also responsible for collecting the royal incomes, for provisioning the castles and their garrisons, and for guarding the prisoners exiled in Malta.

The castles referred to are Mdina and the Castrum Maris (present day Fort St. Angelo). By now the Islands were becoming Christianised and they had some form of representative council through which royal agents of the Sicilian Crown dealt over matters concerning taxation.

In 1249 Frederick II expelled the Muslims from Sicily and Malta, as we have seen, and these were replaced by Christian Latin immigrants. Riccardo de San Germano records that in 1224 the population of Celano from the Abruzzi region of Italy were sent to Malta.

IV) THE ANGEVINS
(1266 - 1282 A.D.)

Frederick II's successors Conrad and Manfred were deposed by the French dynasty of Charles of Anjou, who gained control of Southern

Mdina.

Italy and Sicily. This change had little effect on Malta for the Angevins followed the latter Norman and Swabian policies of exploitation, and the second half of the thirteenth century was a period of particular unrest. It included unwelcome piratical interest in the Islands on the part of the Genoese, Pisans and Venetians.

At the end of Swabian rule, with Manfred in difficulties and the Maltese resentful of German exploitation, a Genoese-inspired rebellion in Malta resulted in all lands and incomes on the Islands belonging to the old Count Henry being devolved on his son Nicoloso.

Charles of Anjou soon restored firm control from Sicily, himself now exploiting the royal lands. Officials collected taxes, and in 1277 the King claimed that his predecessors had received more than 1000 gold *uncie* a year from Malta. There was much resistance to royal taxation and there were petitions against official misappropriations.

Under the Angevins a Captain or Castellan commanded a garrison of trusty French troops and there was a *sagittia* for naval defence, with other vessels to supply the Castrum Maris with victuals from Gozo. There was a public notary who served the two islands, and there were disputes between the Maltese Church and Angevin officials over jurisdictions.

The Islands also suffered from the Angevins' piratical activities. After two Genoese ships were seized at Malta, the Genoese sacked Gozo in 1274 in revenge.
The Maltese Islands were to suffer another Christian attack in 1297 when James II of Aragon ordered his fleet to devastate Malta and Gozo as a gesture against his brother Frederick II of Sicily. It was not only Muslims who attacked Malta.
The Islands were subject to reprisals from any State, be they Christian or Muslim, which happened to be in conflict with Sicily.

V) THE ARAGONESE AND CASTILLIANS (1282-1530 A.D.)

The uprising in Sicily in March 1282, known as the Sicilian Vespers, brought an end to French Angevin rule and established the Spanish Aragonese dynasty. It was Charles of Anjou's ambitions in Byzantium that provoked the uprising and the Aragonese conquest of Sicily. Discontent with harsh Angevin rule the people of

Malta and Gozo welcomed the change in government. Pedro III of Aragon nominated Manfredi Lancia as Captain of Malta and confirmed the privileges by which Costanza and her Swabian son Frederick II had incorporated Malta and Gozo into the royal domain.

But the Angevins were not done. The Castrum Maris held out, and the following year a large fleet from Marseille arrived at Malta to threaten the Aragonese position. The danger soon evaporated as on 8 July 1283 the Aragonese Admiral Ruggiero Lauria won a decisive battle in Malta's Grand Harbour. He was feted by the inhabitants and he left 300 Catalan soldiers behind to hold the Islands.
The Castrum Maris did not fall until the following year.

By 1292 the old claims of the Counts of Malta resurfaced and James of Aragon, now king of Sicily, recognised the Genoese Andreolo as Count of Malta. There followed a period of turmoil in which Malta and Gozo were attacked and devastated by an Aragonese fleet in 1297.
A succession of Maltese Counts followed. Moncada in 1300, and then a batch of d' Aragona princes, Guglielmo, Alfonso by 1330, and Pietro by 1349 at the latest. Pietro

Chapel at Hal Millieri.

lost the County in 1350 when, at their inhabitants' request, Malta and Gozo were returned to the royal domain by King Ludovico of Sicily. The old Maltese nobility dates from this time, though most of the extant titles were created during the latter period of the Order of St. John.

The Maltese were suffering from a clear pattern of events.
The Sicilian King granted them perpetual incorporation in the Crown domain, whilst, at the same time, in periods of stress, granting out the County to absentee and rapacious overlords and royal princes.
This happened again in 1360 when King Frederick of Sicily granted the County of Malta and Gozo to Guido Ventimiglia.
Two years later, however, the Islands again reverted to the Crown.

Further problems for Malta occurred a decade later when King Frederick, supported by ten Genoese galleys, was forced to Malta to oust the troublesome Captain of Malta Giacomo de Pellegrino of Messina from the Castrum Maris in 1372. Another revolt in Malta was provoked by the appointment in

1376 of Giovanni Federigo d'Aragona as Captain of Malta.

Disputed claims to the Crown followed the death of King Frederick in 1377, and the powerful Sicilian magnate Manfredi Chiaramonte put into effect his old claims as Count of Malta. Chiaramonte seized the Tunisian island of Djerba in 1388, and this provoked the Arabs to raid Gozo in 1389.

In spite of all this turmoil an Italian pilgrim on his way to Jerusalem in 1394 noted that the Islands were in a reasonably prosperous state. He mentions that there were 4,000 households in Malta and 400 on Gozo, and talks about the production of cotton, cumin, wine and meat.

King Martin tried to restore royal power in Sicily in the last decade of the 14th century, which sees the appointment of a number of Counts of Malta. In desperation, following decades of oppressive and rebellious Counts, the *Universitates* (people's representatives) of Malta and Gozo yet again petitioned the King for their re-incorporation into the royal domain. Yet again this was granted in perpetuity in 1397.

King Ferdinand (son of King Juan of Castille) was elected the new regent of Sicily in 1412. His son Alphonsus, who succeeded in 1416, was to cost the Maltese dear with his propensity for financing his costly wars at their expense. In 1419, unable to bear further the corsairing raids on the poorly defended Islands, the 'Universita' petitioned Sicily to have a coast watch-tower built on Comino. The plan was approved with the stipulation that a local tax of one florin per barrel of imported wine consumed in Malta and Gozo would be levied to meet the building costs. The tax was collected but found its way into the King's war-depleted coffers. That tower was never built, and Comino remained as a predatory base for assaults on vessels plying between Malta and Gozo. It was not for precisely another two hundred years that a coastal watch tower was built on Comino, during the time of the Knights, and it proved to be the most costly of all in the Islands.Throughout the medieval period the Islands remained practically defenceless, and were subject to constant corsairing attacks and incursions.

In 1420 King Alphonsus pawned the royal incomes from Malta and Gozo to the Sicilian Viceroy Antonio Cardona for 30,000 florins. A renewed pawning in 1426 to Gonsalvo de Monroy provoked immediate outcry, and Monroy's goods were pillaged at Mdina. The Maltese were forced to negotiate with the Crown and were allowed to buy out Monroy. In those hard times they managed to raise 20,000 florins, and the remainder was pardoned on Monroy's death.

The islanders frequently complained of bad weather spoiling the crops, corrupt officials, overtaxation, plagues, invasions and depopulation, and the cost of ransoming back the thousands of Maltese seized by Arab raiders. In 1429, in a devastating raid on Malta, the Tunisian Hafsids carried off

Ossuary in wall of
St. Catherine's church, Zejtun.

more than 3,000 captives. This only ten years after the aborted Comino tower plan.

Following this raid there was a relative peace, but soon a new danger threatened from the East with the expansion of the Turkish Ottomans into the Mediterranean. Malta became a serious objective for the Turks, who attacked Birgu in Malta's Grand Harbour in 1488. The Spanish also had interest in North Africa, and Ferdinand King of Aragon and Sicily captured Tripoli in 1510 with valuable Maltese help.

Malta's sizeable and influential Jewish medieval community was lost to the Islands in 1492, the year of Christopher Colombus, as a result of Ferdinand's royal decree of expulsion of all Jews from all his domains. In order not to lose their property, however, some converted to Christianity and stayed on, contributing to the racial mix that constitutes today's Maltese.

Malta became a bulwark on the southern margin of European Christendom. It lay at the frontiers of a conflict between the western European Spanish Empire and the mighty eastern Ottoman Turks. But it was inadequately defended and exposed to Muslim attacks; Mosta was sacked in 1526.

The Hapsburg Charles V was now King of Spain and Sicily and an ideal opportunity for defending both Malta and Tripoli was presented to him in the form of the Order of St. John.
These Military Hospitaller Knights

had been evicted from Rhodes in 1522/3 by the Turks and were in search of a new home. What a wonderful confluence of interests. Charles V granted Malta and Gozo (as well as Tripoli) in fief to the Order in 1530, and thus commenced a new chapter in the history of the archipelago.

Other than its natural Grand Harbour, there was not much in Malta to impress the Knights. Centuries of exploitative rule from Sicily had allowed little in the way of investment in the Islands. A degree of gracious living could be found in the old citadels, but conditions in the countryside were spartan.
Medieval parish churches were simple box-like structures, not unlike the country chapels in the village of Hal Millieri, where archaeological investigations have provided insight into medieval building technique, burial rite and church decoration.
These churches contained frescoes in an anachronistic Byzantinesque style derived from Sicily. By the time the Knights arrived in Malta the Vatican had already been embellished with the High Renaissance masterpieces of Raphael and Michaelangelo, and the local frescoes must have appeared singularly atavistic to them.
It was the determined programme of investment in the Islands' defences by the Order that allowed the security in which these simple churches could be transformed into the Baroque splendours that they are today.

8. MODERN

I) THE ORDER OF ST. JOHN
(1530 - 1798)

The charitable hospital founded by Amalfi merchants serving pilgrims in Jerusalem was confirmed as a religious order by Pope Paschal II in 1113. This was the time of the Crusades and the Order soon took on the duties of defence of the faith and the Holy Land as well. They were to become known as the Sovereign Military Hospitaller Order of St. John of Jerusalem, Rhodes and Malta - or simply the Order or the Religion. They were driven out of the Holy City by Saladin in 1187, then in 1291 from Acre, and after a

Auberge d'Italie.

Auberge de Castile.

Auberge de Castile.

brief stay in Cyprus took the island of Rhodes from the Byzantines in 1308 (a Christian v. Christian crusade). After withstanding valiantly an Ottoman siege in 1522, the Order's fleet sailed out from Rhodes on the night of January 1st, 1523.

The weakened Order desperately sought help in recapturing Rhodes but the many offers, including one of financial aid from England's Henry VIII in 1528 proved insufficient. They finally had no alternative but to accept Charles V's offer of Malta, albeit a little reluctantly, since a commission sent to the Islands by the Order had reported that both islands and islanders were in a miserable state, the few fortifications were dilapidated and large imports of grain from Sicily were required to feed the population. All this for the nominal annual fee of one Maltese falcon.

The Universita in Mdina did not take kindly to what they saw as yet another broken promise by the King of Sicily going back on his pledge that the Islands would not be given out in fief. The Order set up headquarters in Birgu in the Grand Harbour and established a new Universita there, sidelining traditional Maltese interests at Mdina.
The Order did, however, pledge to uphold the rights and privileges of the Maltese people.

Though still entertaining hopes of returning to Rhodes or finding a base more suitable than Malta the Order set about repairing the Islands' defences and building a couple of new forts, including Fort St. Elmo. The illustrious hero of the Siege of Rhodes, L'Isle Adam, died in 1534, and after a succession of four more Grand Masters, Jean Parisot de La Valette was in place by 1557.

Ottoman raids on Malta continued, that of 1551 being particularly devastating. The Maltese countryside was ravaged and much of the population of Gozo, some 5,000 souls, was carried into slavery. That same year the Knights lost Tripoli.

Auberge de Castile, Valletta
(Now the Prime Minister's office).

By far the largest, most determined and significant Ottoman attack on Malta came in 1565. On May 18 an armada of some 200 vessels arrived off Malta and the following day anchored and disembarked at Marsaxlokk Bay. Main camp was set up at Marsa, at the inner reaches of the Grand Harbour, and it is (over) estimated that there were some 45,000 troops. The smaller local force was led by 540 Knights, and comprised mostly Maltese soldiers, as well as some Italian and Spanish troops, 9,000 in all.

Great deeds of chivalry and brutality on both sides were enacted that summer. Fort St. Elmo fell on June 23rd after an epic struggle of about one month. The Order lost 150 Knights and some 1,500 men, whilst losses on the Turkish side, which included their most able commander Dragut, are estimated at 8,000. Attention then turned to Birgu. On many an occasion the Turks had victory in their grasp but were thwarted by the valiant defenders. Finally, on September 6th, a Christian relief force arrived from Sicily, and two days later a general embarkation of

Fort St. Elmo.

Turkish troops was ordered. The siege was lifted.

This episode, known as The Great Siege, is hailed as one of Malta's most glorious moments. It certainly dented Ottoman aspirations of gaining a foothold in Southern Europe, but it by no means vanquished them. Only six years later a large fleet was mustered by the Ottomans for the Battle of Lepanto.

Though perhaps not decisive, The Great Siege was a glorious victory for Malta, the Order and for Europe. The Order gained increased respect and aid from the European monarchs, and set about putting right the devastated battlefield that Malta had become. After some vacillation, plans for finding an alternative base were forgotten. The Knights stayed on for another two and a half centuries and left their imprint indelibly stamped on the Maltese skyline. During this time the Maltese population increased fivefold, new trades and industries developed and flourished, and renowned artists, military engineers and architects were attracted to the Islands. Malta had never before known such prosperity and sophistication.

The first task in hand was to build a new fortified city. The Pope sent the renowned military engineer Francesco Laparelli to Malta, and his plans transformed the Sceberras peninsula into the city we know today as Valletta, named after the hero of The Great Siege. Grandmaster La Valette laid the foundation stone on 28th March 1566. Spectacular fortifications, grand Auberges, houses, churches and official buildings were erected. This lavish spending provided welcome employment for the Maltese, and ensured that the Knights would not abandon the Islands. The city they built is now a UNESCO World Heritage site, and its fortifications represent a unique example of sixteenth century bastioned European military architecture at its very best.

In time new settlements were established around the Grand Harbour area which became the hub of Malta's commercial activity. Towns in the south of the island expanded but the less easily defended north remained largely underdeveloped. Other than Mdina, that is, where much of Malta's old nobility was ensconced.

Corsairing raids on the Islands continued, and though not as intense or frequent as before, nonetheless posed a constant menace. The Order embarked on a programme of constructing defences for the Islands. Magnificent fortifications encircled the Gozo Castello and Mdina, and the three cities in the Grand Harbour area were ringed by the Cottonera lines. Coastal defences were maintained by the erection of watch towers, redoubts, entrenchments, batteries, fougasses and submarine harbour walls. Forts Manoel, Chambray and

Tigne were built in the final century of the Order's rule.

The Knights were drawn from most of Catholic Europe's noblest families and they brought with them a tradition for the fondness of good taste and high living. Renowned architects, artists and artisans were employed to build and decorate their houses and churches. And this foreign talent rubbed off onto the local artists. The Calabrian painter Mattia Preti was engaged to decorate the Order's Conventual Church of St. John in Valletta, built by the Maltese architect Girolamu Cassar, and he stayed on the island for some forty years until his death in 1699 to paint much else besides. Surely the most renowned artist to have been engaged by the Order was the mercurial Michaelangelo Merisi da Caravaggio, whose two works in St. John's Co-Cathedral constitute Malta's finest artistic treasure. His escape from the dungeons of Fort St. Angelo and flight from the island is shrouded in mystery and intrigue.

The Order was divided into eight Langues, or Tongues, according to the nationality of its members. The

Langues were those of France, Auvergne, Provence, Aragon, Castille, Italy, Germany and England. Each Langue had estates and holdings in their mother countries which financed the Order. (The estates in England were lost when Henry VIII suppressed the English Langue at the time of the dissolution of the monasteries). Corsairing activity including the capture and ransom of slaves was also a significant source of income. Each Langue had its own auberge, or headquarters in Malta, and each Langue was assigned a specific defensive role.

The Order had effective and firm control in Malta. There were, however, two other authorities on the island, namely the Bishop of Malta and the Inquisitor of Malta, with whom friction sometimes arose over the degree of jurisdiction the various authorities had over the

Fort St. Angelo.

R DIOTALLEVIVS
RIMINENSIS
OS. AD A.1608.

LEONETTVS DE CORBARA
ROMANVS
AB A.1608. AD A.1609.

EVANGELISTA CARBO
BONONIENSIS
AB A.1609. AD A.16

TVS NEAPOLITANVS
OA.1728 CREATVS
ALIS DIE IX 7BRIS
43.

FABRITIVS SERBELLONVS MEDIO
LANENSIS AB AN.1728 AD.1730.CR
EATVS S.R.E. CARDINALIS DIE 2 6
9BRIS.1733.

IO. FRANCISCVS STV
DIOLANENSIS AB.AN
CREATVS S.R.E. CAI
DIE 26 9BF

The Inquisitor's Palace, Birgu.

Maltese. As all three bodies owed ultimate allegiance to the Pope, the Holy See was sometimes called in to arbitrate when disputes erupted. Such a dispute occurred over who should have control of censorship of the press when printing was introduced into the Islands in the mid-seventeenth century.

This dispute led to the complete suspension of printing in Malta for a while.

Though early eighteenth century books carry the stamp of having been printed in Malta, they were actually printed in Italy.

The dispute was finally resolved by the granting of the *imprimatur* to all three authorities.

These can be seen printed on the same line (lest one might appear to have precedence over another) in I. S. Mifsud's "Biblioteca Maltese" of 1764.

Two Inquisitors of Malta went on to become Pope, and many received the Cardinal's hat.

Although sworn to vows of chastity and obedience the occasional Knight might stray into lawlessness, unruly behaviour and wenching, or even heresy. There was no lack of candidates for the Order's dungeons.

The raison d'etre of the Order had become its crusading role, the defence of Christendom. But they never forgot the original purpose for which they were founded - the caring of the sick. One of their first acts on taking up residence in Birgu had been to establish a hospital there, and in the new city of Valletta they built the splendid Sacred Infirmary, which today is known as the Mediterranean Conference Centre. This hospital, where patients were served with silver platters, achieved fame as being one of the finest in Europe, and Maltese surgeons and physicians gained international recognition. It was here that the School of Anatomy and Malta's University was founded in 1769.

During the Order's rule the Maltese population grew from something like 20,000 to 100,000. Of course

Mdina Cathedral.

Fort St. Angelo, Birgu.

there were occasional blips such as the plague of 1675-6 which carried off some 10,000 of the 60,000 population. Villages and towns grew larger and vied with each other for the splendour of their Baroque churches. Many of these were built by the Maltese architect Lorenzo Gafa', who is also responsible for the Gozo and Mdina Cathedrals, the latter replacing its Romanesque predecessor damaged in the 1693 earthquake. Meanwhile Lorenzo's brother Melchior, the sculptor, had achieved international fame in Bernini's Rome.

The Order provided the stability in Malta necessary for growth and investment. They were its largest economic unit, its major source of income and employment; just as

Coast watch tower.

the British, in their time, would become. It was the income earned from the Order's European properties that drove the Maltese economy. And the input from the private family fortunes of individual Knights financed much of the Order's building programme. Grandmaster Alof de Wignacourt (1601 - 1622) for example, contributed half a million scudi to the Order's coffers, personally paying for an aqueduct to provide Valletta with an adequate water supply, and also constructing a number of coastal fortresses, including that on Comino. Martin de Redin (1657 - 1660) built thirteen coastal watchtowers around the Islands, whilst Antoine Manoel de Vilhena (1722 - 1736) of Fort Manoel Island fame, was another generous benefactor.

The Order's shipbuilding yard in Birgu provided employment, as of course did the boon given to the building industry, although sometimes slaves, even those in private employ, were pressed into this kind of work. The cotton industry, already in place in the Middle Ages, flourished during the Order's rule, and became one of the most important commodities of the export trade. All sorts of trades and crafts flourished, the gold and silversmiths earning a particularly good reputation.

However, a good deal of material had to be imported from Europe, mostly via Sicilian ports, and most importantly wheat. Barbary corsairs sometimes disrupted these supplies, though Malta under the Order was not unknown to trade with Muslim states, such as when importing wheat from Tunis. Malta-based shipping itself was involved in corsairing and the *corso* was a profitable industry, with Maltese crew mainly manning the privateers.

Other than inanimate goods the *corso* also provided captive slaves

Torri l'Ahmar.

for one of Europe's biggest slave markets - Malta.

In terms of numbers, however, farming remained Malta's principal industry. The land had been devastated in 1565, so under the Order's rule agriculture had to be rehabilitated. Grain was a major crop, though wheat always had to be imported. Cotton, the main export commodity, was often grown at the expense of wheat. Its seed was also used as feed for animal stock, so cotton occupied a central role in rural life. Cumin after which the island of Comino takes its name, was also exported in considerable quantity.

Maltese citrus fruits, particularly oranges, enjoyed a high reputation. Cattle and pigs were the major source of meat, whilst the large herds of goats were the principal sources of milk. Being less densely populated than Malta, Gozo was able to ship daily boatloads of agricultural produce to the larger

island.

In spite of the relative stability and prosperity the Order brought to the Islands, there were some in 18th century Malta who began to see them as philandering despotic rulers. An uprising of a group of discontents led by the clergy in 1775 was quickly put down. But a more serious threat to the Order was looming. The menace of Ottoman aspirations in Europe was on the decline, and so, therefore, was the role of the Order as the defender of Christendom. European powers began to look askance at the vast sums of money pouring into the Islands, and none more so than revolutionary France, from where the bulk of it came. In 1792 the Revolution confiscated all possessions in France of the religious and aristocratic Order. From then on the Order ceased to be an economically viable Government, and its demise became only a matter of time. Discontent grew, and another attempt at overthrow of the Knights by the Maltese was uncovered in 1797. Some of the ringleaders were condemned to death and others

Żabbar Gate.

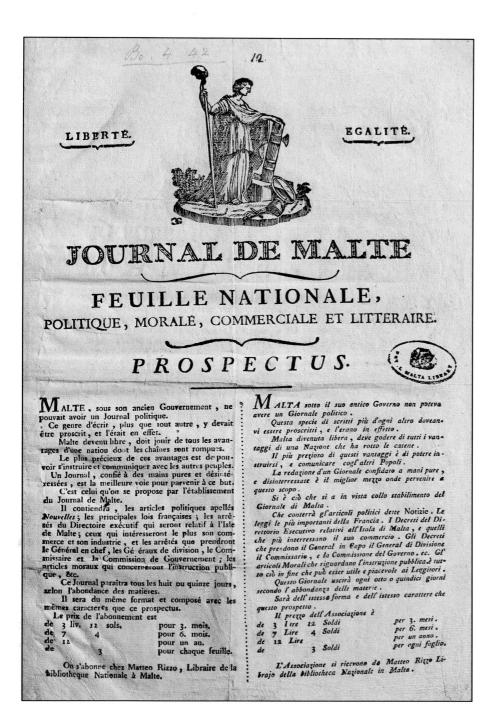

JOURNAL DE MALTE

FEUILLE NATIONALE,
POLITIQUE, MORALE, COMMERCIALE ET LITTERAIRE.

PROSPECTUS.

MALTE, sous son ancien Gouvernement, ne pouvait avoir un Journal politique.

Ce genre d'écrit, plus que tout autre, y devait être proscrit, et l'était en effet.

Malte devenu libre, doit jouir de tous les avantages d'une nation dont les chaînes sont rompues.

Le plus précieux de ces avantages est de pouvoir s'instruire et communiquer avec les autres peuples.

Un Journal, confié à des mains pures et désintéressées, est la meilleure voie pour parvenir à ce but.

C'est celui qu'on se propose par l'établissement du Journal de Malte.

Il contiendra, les articles politiques appellés *Nouvelles*; les principales lois françaises; les arrêtés du Directoire exécutif qui seront relatif à l'Isle de Malte; ceux qui intéresseront le plus son commerce et son industrie, et les arrêtés que prendront le Général en chef, les Généraux de division, le Commissaire et la Commission de Gouvernement; les articles moraux qui concerneront l'instruction publique, &c.

Ce Journal paraîtra tous les huit ou quinze jours, selon l'abondance des matières.

Il sera du même format et composé avec les mêmes caractères que ce prospectus.

Le prix de l'abonnement est

de 3 liv. 12 sols,	pour 3. mois.
de 7 4	pour 6. mois.
de 12	pour un an.
de 3	pour chaque feuille.

On s'abonne chez Matteo Rizzo, Libraire de la bibliothèque Nationale à Malte.

MALTA sotto il suo antico Governo non poteva avere un Giornale politico.

Questa specie di scritti più d'ogni altro doveano vi essere proscritti, e l'erano in effetto.

Malta divenuta libera, deve godere di tutti i vantaggi di una Nazione che ha rotto le catene.

Il più prezioso di questi vantaggi è di potere instruirsi, e comunicare cogl'altri Popoli.

La redazione d'un Giornale confidata a mani pure, e disinterressate è il miglior mezzo onde pervenire a questo scopo.

Si è ciò che si a in vista collo stabilimento del Giornale di Malta.

Che conterrà gl'articoli politici dette Notizie. Le leggi le più importanti della Francia. I Decreti del Direttorio Esecutivo relativi all'Isola di Malta, e quelli che più interressano il suo commercio. Gli Decreti che prendono il General in Capo il General di Divisione il Commissario, e la Commissione del Governo. ec. Gl'articoli Morali che riguardano l'instruzione pubblica tutto ciò in fine che può esser utile e piacevole ai Leggitori.

Questo Giornale uscirà ogni otto o quindici giorni secondo l'abbondanza delle materie.

Sarà dell'istessa forma e dell'istesso carattere che questo prospetto.

Il prezzo dell'Associazione è

de 3 Lire 12 Soldi	per 3. mesi.
de 7 Lire 4 Soldi	per 6. mesi.
de 12 Lire	per un anno.
de 3 Soldi	per ogni foglio.

L'Associazione si ricevono da Matteo Rizzo Librajo della bibliotheca Nazionale in Malta.

French newspaper in Malta.

exiled. Mikiel Anton Vassalli (who was probably buried in the British Msida Bastion Cemetery) was sentenced to life imprisonment in Fort Ricasoli.

Anticipating the interest of England, Russia and Austria in failing Malta, Napoleon Bonaparte appeared off the island on June 9th 1798. The Order was softened by fifth columnist French Knights; with the fortifications being poorly manned

and the Maltese undesirous of doing battle with the French, it capitulated within a few days. It is ironic that after all the lavish spending and preparations the fortifications were given up with scarce a shot being fired in anger. Napoleon landed at Customs House Wharf on the afternoon of June 12th and marched into Valletta via Del Monte's gate (since replaced by Victoria Gate) preceded by a French military band. He took up

residence at Palazzo Parisio in Merchants Street, next door to the Auberge de Castille.

Grandmaster Ferdinand von Hompesch and a bevy of knights with a few of their movable possessions sailed ignominiously out of Grand Harbour.

II) THE FRENCH (1798 - 1800)

Napoleon only remained in Malta for six days, though judging by the number of beds he is reputed to have slept in, and desks sat at, it would seem like an eternity. General Vaubois was left behind in command of about 4,000 troops.

The French, initially welcomed by some on the island, immediately set about instituting reforms according to their revolutionary principles. Slavery and the nobility were abolished, heraldic escutcheons were defaced and freedom of the press was established. Political prisoners, including the priest Mannarino who had been incarcerated for his part in the 1775 uprising, were released. The Order's wealth on the Islands was plundered, and their debts to local merchants and pensions to loyal servants went unpaid. New taxes were introduced and hardship began to mount.

All this might have been tolerated, but the Maltese were not prepared to put up with the French Republican assault on the Catholic Church (a mistake the British subsequently took pains, though not always successfully, to avoid). Politically foolish anticlerical measures hardened the Maltese attitude against the French, whose position in Malta was weakened by news of the Royal Navy's routing of

Napoleon's fleet in Aboukir Bay on August 24th. Things came to a head on September 2nd as the French were stripping the Franciscan church in Rabat, and the Carmelite church in Mdina. The Maltese massacred the French garrison in Mdina and within hours the rebellion had spread throughout the Islands. The insurgents soon took the countryside and Vaubois was confined to the fortified areas around the Grand Harbour. Vaubois complained "We had to combat enraged lions..........."

Emmanuele Vitale, and Vincenzo Borg (Brared) were prominent leaders after the uprising. A Maltese National Assembly was formed and sent for help from Sicily and the British fleet. Nelson despatched a detachment under Captain Alexander Ball and himself appeared in October to take stock. Ball was commanded to blockade the French into starving submission, and was eventually also recognised

A typical Maltese balcony, Valletta.

Palazzo Parisio, Valletta.

by the Maltese as the spokesman for their cause. Vaubois determined to resist "till the last sack of grain". The Gozo Castello, still in French hands, capitulated on October 28th, 1798 and the British flag was run up. Nelson departed, and a bitter siege that was to last almost two years ensued, causing much

disruption and hardship in the Islands.
The Maltese were poorly armed and short of money and food, and several attempts at taking the fortified towns around Grand Harbour proved unsuccessful. Conditions for the besieged were appalling. A plot within Valletta

was uncovered and about fifty-four Maltese insurrectionists, including the priest Mikiel Xerri, were executed early in 1799. Disease, hunger and military action were taking their toll of both sides, and in the summer of 1800 the domestic animals and rats of Valletta were all consumed. The French could hold out no longer and after a valiant defence, Vaubois capitulated on September 5th to Major General Pigot, commander of the British land forces aiding the Maltese. Ball, who represented the Maltese, was excluded from the negotiations.

Other than the defaced escutcheons (most of which have since been replaced), practically the only other tangible reminder of French rule is a dimly faded street sign, protected by a perspex slab, that survives on a corner column just in front of the National Library in Valletta.

III) THE BRITISH (1800 - 1964)

Somewhat to their surprise, the British found themselves de facto rulers of Malta by right of conquest. Ball was put in charge as Civil Commissioner (in 1804 he had Samuel Taylor Coleridge as his Private Secretary). The Order and the Kingdom of Sicily still laid claim to the Islands, and of course the Maltese themselves were interested in determining their own future. In 1802 a Maltese deputation in London requested that the Islands be placed under the permanent protection of His Britannic Majesty. The British soon realised the importance of Malta as

One of the Gardens set up by Ball.

a naval and trading base in the Mediterranean, and as an important outwork to India, though an outbreak of plague in 1813 put a halt to trading activities for some time.

In 1812 a Commission was sent out from England to report on the state of affairs and to make recommendations for the future. The Commission noted that there was some discontent with British rule in the higher orders of society, though "the great mass and body of the people were happy and contented", but "whose habits, customs, religion and education are in direct opposition to our own". The Commissioners noted that any interference with the local Church, its courts and special privileges would "draw down the indignation of an angry priesthood". Much to the indignation of local politicians it was not considered expedient to set up a *consiglio popolare* or form of local government.

Sir Thomas Maitland was sent out as first Governor of Malta in the midst of the 1813 plague. The determined measures he took to control the outbreak were to characterise his iron rule for the next eleven years. The autocratic manner in which he reorganised the Islands' administrative institutions earned him the sobriquet 'King Tom'.

International legal recognition of British possession of Malta came in 1814 with the signing of the Treaty of Paris by the European powers.

Britain consolidated its position in Malta. The garrison was increased

in numbers and the Order's fortifications were repaired and improved. Initially the British had no need to build new fortifications. The Islands' defences had been more than adequately catered for by the Knights; it was just a question of manning them and having the will to defend them, a qualification that was found lacking in the last days of the Order.

The first structures built by the British in Malta were in the Neo-Classical style, a style as yet virtually unknown in the predominantly Baroque islands. It was the style that represented the Empire's growing Imperial glory, and the style that was utilised for Ball's cenotaph in the Lower Barrakka Gardens after his death in 1809. This was the first sepulchral monument on the Islands since ancient times to be erected in a public place and not in a church setting, and it set the trend for nineteenth century architecture in British Malta. Other Neo-Classical sepulchral monuments were set up in the Upper Barrakka Gardens, in the Msida Bastion Cemeteries and elsewhere. The portico of the old University and of the main guard in Palace Square, the exedra in Fort St. Elmo and the folly at Villa Frere were all done in this style.

The first substantial building erected by the British in Malta was the Neo-Classical Bighi Naval Hospital, an 1830 conversion and expansion of Lorenzo Gafa's Bichi Palace. The memorials and buildings set up by the British proclaimed the new order to the Maltese populace. Britannia rejected the Catholic counter-reformation

Baroque style. The Auberge of Germany was demolished and replaced by the Neo-Classical Ionic temple St. Paul's Anglican Cathedral, consecrated in 1844. Its Neo-Gothic bell-tower, and the Protestant memorials to Spencer and Ponsonby, reaching up to pierce the heavens, disturbed the typical Maltese skyline of flat-topped houses and hemispherical Baroque domes. Britannia ruled the waves.

In 1848 the first British admiralty dry dock was opened. Malta became established as a major base for the Royal Navy, which utilised its services in the Crimean War of 1853-56. The opening of the Suez Canal in 1869 had important consequences for Malta as it placed the Islands on the major Imperial seaway to India and beyond. Malta was the headquarters of the British Mediterranean fleet, and its strategic importance was reflected in the second half of the nineteenth century by the construction of new fortresses, defences, barracks, military hospitals and improvements to the harbours and dockyard.

All this activity was healthy for the economy, but it was not all plain sailing. Following the plague of 1813 the economy had stagnated and the cholera epidemic of 1837 carried off another 4,000 lives. But after that population growth accelerated. In 1851 there were 123,494 persons living on the Islands, by 1871 there were over 140,000 and some 200,000 by the turn of the century. Overpopulation

Bighi Naval Hospital.

became a problem, and though the British services provided much employment, recourse to emigration was sought by the unemployed. By the end of the nineteenth century there were well over 50,000 Maltese dispersed in communities around the shores of the Mediterranean. They were principally situated in Algeria, Tunis, Tripoli and Egypt, but were also to be found in scattered communities in Gibraltar, Sicily, the Ionian Islands and Turkey.

Agriculture, so important to the Maltese economy, underwent a number of changes under the British. Sir Alexander Ball had introduced the potato to the Islands and it eventually became a staple crop and one of the major exports. But efforts to introduce a silk industry failed, and other than a brief spurt provided by the American Civil War, the cultivation of cotton also declined in the nineteenth century. The land was given over to the new potato crop, wheat and *sulla*, a kind of clover which replaced cotton seed as feed for the animals. New areas of agricultural land, particularly in the north of Malta, were now brought under cultivation by improved methods of irrigation.

St. Paul's Anglican Cathedral, Spire.

The Royal Navy expanded the Order's old shipyard. Following the first dry dock opened in Dockyard Creek in 1848, the huge Somerset Dock was opened in French Creek in 1871, to be followed by another three on the same site. The Grand Harbour became the chief coaling station for vessels plying between Britain and the East, and all this provided much needed employment. But the economy was too heavily based on agriculture and services provided by the British Military and Naval establishment. These were subject to fluctuations, and there was practically no investment in productive industry. There were times of prosperity and times of hardship.

Constitutionally Malta also suffered a chequered history. Having freely and voluntarily sought the permanent protection of Britain and recognised the King of Great Britain as their Sovereign, the Maltese were lumped with 'King Tom' Maitland as their first Governor under the new

Crown Colony system in 1813. All power was in his hands and the Maltese were denied any system of representation. This was regarded as unfair and treacherous of the British. After all, the Maltese had spilled their blood in evicting the French, and had a long tradition of representation in the form of the *Universita* or *Consiglio Popolare*. It was a retrograde step.

Following the strenuous efforts of the Maltese leader George Mitrovich and the British Parliamentarian William Ewart as well as two petitions presented to the House of Commons, a Council was constituted in Malta in 1835 "to advise and assist in the administration of the Government thereof". The seven man Council had three Maltese members, including the Bishop, who, on advice from the Vatican, declined his seat. It was only advisory, the Governor retaining overall control, and there was no provision for elective representation. Its composition was subsequently altered. A momentous Ordinance passed by this Council of Government in March 1839 introduced freedom of the press, contrary to the wishes of most in the Church, and established a law of libel. This new law was immediately put to the test when the Protestant newspaper THE HARLEQUIN was found guilty of reviling the Catholic Religion.

Drydocks.

*British military
Barracks.*

*Military
Cemetery.*

A new constitution in 1849 enlarged the Council of Government to eighteen members, ten official and eight elected members. This Council had the power to legislate, but the Governor retained the power to act over its head if he deemed it necessary. The official members had control and the Maltese elected members had no effective say in domestic matters or supply of public moneys, for which they clamoured. This grievance caused political unrest and the Maltese resorted to the deliberate election of simpletons and undesirables to the Council with the object "of bringing the Council of Government under contempt", as the Secretary of State fully realised.

Reforms in the administrative, fiscal and educational fields suggested by the British helped crystallise the body of Maltese political opinion into two camps. The 'Language Question' played a significant part in this, and was to dominate local politics until the outbreak of the Second World War.

On one side were the 'anti-reformists', championed by Fortunato Mizzi who represented the traditionalist pro-Italian culture wing.
They were opposed to the teaching of English at the expense of Italian in Maltese schools, as suggested in the reforms. They were also against the proposed reforms in the system of taxation and in the Civil Service. They were the genesis of the Nationalist Party. Their promotion of the Italian language, coupled with the nationalistic movement in neighbouring Italy caused concern to the British rulers.

On the other side were the pro-reform group exemplified by people like Sigismondo Savona, the Director of Education, who tended to be pro-English and in favour of the educational and other reforms.

A new constitution was introduced in 1887 "designed - to give to the representatives of the people of Malta, for the first time, a specific power of deciding questions of finance and other questions of local concern, while full power is reserved to the Crown......", as stated by the Secretary of State for the colonies. The elected members on the Council of twenty had a majority.

By the turn of the century the language question had become

The National Library, Valletta.

acute. The majority of Maltese of course spoke Maltese. Many of the middle and upper classes, a minority, used Italian for professional and business purposes, and often, also, in everyday speech, as they had done since pre-Colonial times. As many Maltese became dependent on the British services for their livelihood it naturally became advantageous for them to be proficient in English. The British, also to their advantage, encouraged the introduction of the teaching of English on a free choice policy, allowing parents to choose the language (English or Italian) in which they wished their children to be instructed. The elected Maltese members of the Council, on the other hand, advocated a pari-passu policy, implying the simultaneous teaching of both languages. The Maltese language itself was drawn into the equation, gaining backing from the British, but earning the disapproval of the anti-reformists.

The burning issue of the language question was underscored by political considerations. Simplistically put, the pro-Italians were anti-British with the implication of closer ties with Italy. The other side was pro-Britain and Empire. In reality it was more about who governs, and who *decides* what language to use, be it English, Italian, Maltese or Japanese for that matter. This was a period of conflict and elected members were now representing a growing nationalistic movement calling for self-government. The 1887 constitution had become unworkable. The elected members had power without responsibility. They could obstruct the machinery of Government, but did not bear the executive responsibility for their actions.

In 1903 the elected members rejected the education estimates for that financial year, bringing the system to a halt. The British responded by revoking the 1887 constitution and instituted a new Council of Government. It was not self-government, but a reversal to the 1849 situation where the official

members had the majority. It elicited strong protest from the elected members, but official majority rule lasted until 1921.

It should be remembered that at the turn of the century there was no popular franchise and few people were involved in the political process. Out of a population of some 200,000 only an elite 10,000 had the vote, and many of these abstained from casting it. It was by no means all conflict between the British and Maltese, who generally enjoyed cordial relations. A section of the population, indeed, became quite anglicised.

The Maltese were united however, with only a few notable exceptions, on the question of religion. Conscious of this, the British trod a wary path, though occasionally got into trouble. When planning burial reform in the late 1860's it was proposed to set up a new multi-denominational public cemetery. This provoked a public outcry. The Catholic clergy would not consecrate ground in which Protestants would also be laid to rest. It was reported to London "The Maltese are happy to sit at table at the Palace with their wives and daughters, but would not deign to share their final resting place with their guests". Two separate cemeteries were established, the Addolorata for Catholics and Ta' Braxia for Protestants.

The beginning of the twentieth century saw the economy on the decline with unemployment rising, in some part due to diminished Naval expenditure in Malta at the expense of the Home Fleet. Germany was building up its Navy. The First World War was a mixed blessing economically and Malta, with her hospital facilities, acted as 'Nurse of the Mediterranean'. The

end of the War saw renewed unemployment and economic difficulties, with the price of bread rising. Political agitation also increased, and a newly formed National Assembly, gathered to voice the political aspirations of the Maltese, called for the British Government to grant a constitution "with full political and administrative autonomy".

As a result of the prevailing political and economic unrest riots broke out on 7th June 1919 in which four Maltese were killed when troops opened fire. No doubt this was one of the factors borne in mind in 1921 when Secretary of State Winston Churchill submitted to the Governor, Lord Plumer, instructions for a new constitution which provided for "the establishment of responsible government, subject to certain limitations". The Maltese had self-government in matters of local concern, whilst the British retained control in matters of Imperial concern.

The Maltese set about ruling themselves and again it proved a fractious business. There ensued hotly contested and passionate debates, both in and out of Parliament, between the pro-British and pro-Italian factions. Lord Strickland's pro-British group felt the ire of the pro-Italian Nationalists who had the backing of the Church, and Strickland himself was no mean combatant. The old language question was at the fore.

The conflict caused the British Government to suspend the constitution in 1930. Although it was restored two years later it was again suspended in 1933, and Malta did not regain internal self-government until 1947.

The British, now in full control

again, settled the language question once and for all. In 1934 Maltese was made the official language of the Courts in preference to Italian. The majority of litigants could now understand what was being said, in their native tongue. In 1936 English and Maltese became the official languages of Malta, English being used for administrative purposes and Maltese in the Courts. The teaching of English and Maltese came to occupy a more important place in the schools' curricula. And so it has remained.

Royal Air Force memorial, Floriana.

But the Italian language continued to be a rallying point for Nationalist politicians who deemed the British to be eroding their traditional culture. The Italian fascists of the 1930's supported their cause and the British suspected that there were some in Malta who were leaning towards irredentist aspirations.

When the Second World War broke out these men were interned, and in 1942 a group of forty-three Maltese nationals was deported to Uganda at His Majesty's pleasure. During an impassioned plea in their defence in Parliament, the Nationalist Sir Ugo Mifsud collapsed, and died two days later. They were a motley crew comprising a Chief Justice, a prominent politician, professionals and others more humble. They had committed no crime, nor were they convicted of any. Such are the exigencies of war. Thankfully they all returned safely after the war, three to be elected to Parliament, one of their number becoming Prime Minister.

Malta was ill prepared for war. When Italy joined the fray on June 11th 1940 she attacked Malta the same day with a wave of bomber aircraft and lost much of her local sympathy. The Royal Malta Artillery lost six of its anti-aircraft gunners. The Islands' air defences consisted of just four Sea Gloster Gladiator fighter planes and that first day they brought down an Italian aircraft. One was soon lost, and the remaining three, dubbed "Faith", "Hope" and "Charity", were left to soldier on against the two hundred Italian planes in Sicily.

This second siege of Malta had much in common with the Great Siege of 1565. The island was poorly prepared for battle, the odds were stacked against her, the

Maltese population played a significant role, and deeds of heroism were enacted on both sides.

Hurricane fighters were brought in to replace the Gladiators, and torpedo and bomber aircraft also found their way to Malta and made effective raids on Italian seaports and shipping. Following the rout of the Italians in North Africa the Luftwaffe moved into Sicily in December and the bombing of Malta intensified. In January 1941 the crippled aircraft carrier H.M.S. Illustrious was in Grand Harbour being refitted when the Germans launched a thunderous blitz with sixty-one Junker bombers escorted by fifty fighter planes. The brunt of the attack was borne by the three harbour cities and Valletta, where many people and homes were lost. When Hitler attacked Russia in late June 1941 some pressure on Malta was relieved due to the redeployment of much of the Luftwaffe.

Although short of supplies Malta now began bombing and

torpedoeing the vital Axis supply shipping serving Rommel in North Africa. On the other hand, Axis submarines were very active in attacking British convoys bringing much needed supplies to the beleaguered island.

In July 1941 the Italians made a daring but abortive night attack on the shipping in Grand Harbour. Using small explosive motor boats, or E-boats, they failed to penetrate into Grand Harbour. Some were blown up in the attempt, others were picked off by shore batteries, and those that managed to flee were sunk or crippled by Hurricanes.

Malta suffered its most intense and sustained period of bombing between December 1941 and May 1942 when over 10,000 tons of bombs were unloaded on the Islands. The densely populated areas around the Grand Harbour suffered the heaviest casualties. In all, the bombing sustained by Malta destroyed some 35,000 houses and numerous public buildings and monuments, including the Royal

Opera House in Valletta whose ruins to this day remain as an eloquent reminder of those belligerent times.

Civilian war deaths (not including those attached to the military), some 1,500, were kept to a minimum by evacuation from the dockyard and harbour areas to the countryside. Innumerable rock-cut shelters were constructed, and old railway tunnels and catacombs were also utilised for shelter. The disruption to life was made more severe by the acute shortage of food.

The air defences of Malta were shorn up by Spitfires flown in from aircraft carriers, and by July 1st there were over 200 aircraft in operation, over 100 of them being Spitfires. An Axis plan to attack and capture Malta failed to materialise, and though the bombing continued, the agile and speedy Spitfires were better able to deal with enemy aircraft. Nonetheless they suffered heavy casualties.

By the summer of 1942 the Islands were close to starvation and military supplies such as aviation fuel were also at critically low levels. Operation Pedestal was launched against this background. A convoy of 14 merchant vessels under heavy escort entered the Mediterranean on August 10th, bound for Malta. These brave men suffered heavy casualties from Axis air, sea and submarine attack. On August 13th three merchantmen limped into Grand Harbour to a delirious welcome. The Brisbane Star came in the following day, and on August 15th the legendary Ohio, decks almost awash, rudderless, and carrying vital fuel, oil and kerosene, was nudged into French Creek to rapturous applause. Malta was saved by the heroic deeds of the men of the "Santa Maria Convoy".

This was a tremendous boost for morale, and though the air raids continued they began to decrease in number, and the outlook improved. Malta proved crucial to

The Breakwater, Grand Harbour.

the battle for North Africa by squeezing the Axis supply lines. One and a half million tons of enemy shipping were sunk. The British victory at El Alamein in late October was decisive and by May 1943 all Africa was in Allied hands and hostilities in Malta practically came to an end. Sicily was invaded on 10th July and Malta was the operational headquarters for the launch of the attack. The Italian Armistice was signed on 8th September, and twenty-eight ships of the Italian fleet were brought to Maltese harbours.

The war in Malta was over, though the last "all clear" air raid siren was not sounded until 9 p.m. on 28th August 1944. The servicemen and civilians had acquitted themselves admirably in the fight against Nazism and Fascism. In a message to the Governor of Malta from Buckingham Palace on 15th April 1942 King George VI had written: "To honour her brave people I award the George Cross to the Island Fortress of Malta to bear witness to a heroism and devotion that will long be famous in history".

Malta ended the war with an acute housing shortage due to the bombing, and a War Damage Grant of £30 million by the British Government helped finance reconstruction. The end of hostilities also brought unemployment and emigration on a substantial scale was organised to Australia, North America and to a lesser extent the U.K.

In 1947 Malta was granted a new constitution which restored self-government on the lines of that of

War Memorial, Floriana.

1921. A Legislative Assembly of forty members drawn from eight constituencies was set up, and for the first time, universal suffrage was introduced. The old sex, education and property qualifications disappeared, and all over the age of twenty-one were eligible to vote. English and Maltese were confirmed as the official languages of the Islands.

The newly elected Labour Government had the young Dom Mintoff as Minister of Public Works and Reconstruction, and he proved to be a dominating presence in local politics for the next half century. He fell out with his Prime Minister Dr. Paul Boffa, and the Nationalists under Dr. Enrico Mizzi (a returned deportee), formed the government after the 1950 elections. After two more coalition governments headed by the Nationalist Dr. Giorgio Borg Olivier, Dom Mintoff's Labour Party obtained a majority in the 1955 elections. Borg Olivier's proposals for Dominion Status in 1953 had floundered, and Mintoff now came up with the idea of Integration with Britain whereby Malta would be represented by three members in the House of Commons. This idea found favour with the British, but it was opposed by the Nationalists and strongly opposed by the local Catholic Church, which was fearful of Protestant influences integration might bring to the staunchly Catholic islands. A national referendum on the issue was held in 1956, and the Church is credited with ensuring that the necessary majority vote (of ALL registered voters) required for integration was not obtained. The Nationalists boycotted the referendum, and though the majority of those who cast their vote were in favour of integration, this was not enough.

By now Mintoff's relations were strained not only with the Church, but also with the British Government, and his administration resigned in 1958. The Governor assumed powers to maintain law and order, and the Constitution was revoked in 1959. Malta was now run by an Executive Council.

In 1961 self-government was restored by the granting of a new constitution and a Nationalist administration under Borg Olivier was returned in the February 1962 elections, not without help from the Church. The Prime Minister soon wrote to the Secretary of State demanding "for the Maltese Islands' independence within the Commonwealth". The Malta Independence Conference was held at Marlborough House, London, in July 1963, and following further discussions and consultations it was decided to hold a referendum on the proposed constitution. Approval came in May 1964 and the Malta Independence Act, passed by the United Kingdom Parliament received royal assent on 31st July 1964.

IV) INDEPENDENT MALTA

Independence took effect on "the appointed day" of September 21st 1964. Malta remained in the Commonwealth with the Queen of Britain as Head of State and represented by a Governor General on the island.

Independence statue at Floriana.

Political independence had been achieved, but many were preoccupied with Malta's prospects of gaining economic independence. The new State entered into an agreement on mutual defence and assistance with Great Britain whose government undertook to provide Malta with £50 million (part loan) over a period of ten years in return for the use of military facilities. British troops remained on the island.

Traditionally dependent on British Services spending, Malta now had to diversify its economy. New manufacturing industries were set up and tourism encouraged. From a figure of 40,000 in 1964 the annual number of tourists visiting the Islands rose to 170,000 by 1970 (and at the turn of the century it has topped the 1 million mark).

In 1967 Britain announced massive and rapid cuts in the number of jobs available to Maltese at the British defence establishments on the Islands, which were also to be curtailed. After a somewhat tense period the British Government agreed to slow down the timetable for the proposed run down, but the episode served as a salient reminder of Malta's lingering dependence on Britain's military base.

Dom Mintoff's Labour Party won the elections in 1971 and he soon informed the British Government that the defence and assistance agreement would be cancelled unless it was substantially revised in Malta's favour. Britain was unimpressed. But Mintoff was a shrewd and tough negotiator and played on NATO's fears that Malta might instead become a base for hostile forces. After a protracted series of negotiations, agreement was reached in 1972 that Malta was to receive an annual payment of £14 million per annum from combined UK and other NATO sources in return for the use of military facilities on the island.

These increased financial resources helped the Government to expand the economy, and to make the Islands, eventually, independent of income derived directly from military bases.

A landmark constitutional change was effected in December 1974 when Malta became a Republic with a Maltese President as Head of State. Malta retained its membership of the Commonwealth.

Other than the consideration of making Malta economically independent of military bases, the Labour Party also pursued a foreign policy of neutrality and non-alignment. On 31st March 1979 the military base agreement was terminated and the last British

Bush/Gorbachev Meeting, Marsaxlokk, 1989.

servicemen left the island. In 1981 Malta deposited a Declaration of Neutrality with the United Nations, and in 1987 an amendment declaring Malta to be a neutral State was entrenched in the Constitution.

The 1987 elections returned the Nationalist Party headed by Eddie Fenech Adami. On historical, cultural, political and economic considerations the Nationalist Party see Malta's role to be firmly within Europe. With this goal in mind the Government formally applied for full membership of the European Union and initiated negotiations for membership. Domestically the Government's policy included gearing the economy and relative legislation towards conformity with European standards in anticipation of membership.

Having reached an advanced stage in negotiations with the Union, the Nationalist Party lost the 1996 election to Labour's Alfred Sant. The new Government, though maintaining a policy of close co-operation with the Union, did not deem full membership to be advisable, and froze Malta's application. But the Government was short-lived and was brought down when the irascible Dom Mintoff, now a back-bencher, crossed the floor of the House on a vote linked to a confidence motion.

Birgu, British Troops Departure Monument 1979.

Independence and Republic day Memorial Plaques.

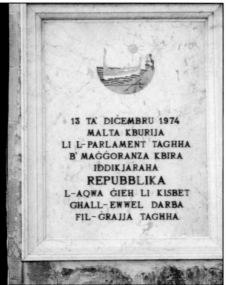

The Nationalist Party were returned in the subsequent 1998 elections and have re-activated Malta's application for full membership of the European Union. When negotiations for conditions of entry have been completed the Maltese people will decide in a Referendum whether or not they wish to join the Union.

VALLETTA MUSEUMS

The best way to see Valletta is to wander around on foot. Explore the side streets, and don't forget to look up occasionally and take in the architectural details of the Baroque buildings. You will encounter numerous statue niches on street corners and individual houses; forgotten fountains and many other surprises. Pop into any church you come across. Don't fail to go to the Upper Barrakka Gardens and savour the spectactular view over Grand Harbour. Some of the principal museums of Valletta are described below. Not included is the Mediterranean Conference Centre (the old Hospital of the Order) which is worth a visit, and where "The Malta Experience" is shown nearby. The audio-visuals give a good summary of Malta's history. Another audio-visual show in valletta is "The Great Siege of Malta and The Knights of St. John" sited in the Café' Premier Complex on the ground floor of the National Library. The 45 minutes experience takes the visitor on a journey of a thousand years from the inception of the order, Crusading times to the present day.

NATIONAL MUSEUM OF FINE ART

Located in South Street, this museum exhibits the pick of the national collection. It is housed in a magnificent 18th century late Baroque palace known as 'Casa Maira' which was used in British times as Admiralty House. Don't overlook the architectural details of this gracious building, particularly its elegant staircase.

The collection is arranged in a series of rooms on two floors in chronological order allowing the visitor to experience the evolution of Western European art from the 14th century down to modern times. The upper floor (Rooms 1 - 13) displays works from the 14th to the 17th centuries, whilst the ground floor is devoted to works of the subsequent three centuries.

The medieval decorative Gothic style in Room 1, as exemplified by the "Flagellation" scene, gives way to 15th and 16th century Renaissance and Mannerist works in the following rooms. Room 3 is dedicated to the Florentine version of these styles, as exemplified by Filippo Paladini's "Mystic Marriage of St. Catherine", whilst the Venetian experience is displayed in Room 4, as in Andrea Vicentino's "Raising of Lazarus". Dutch, Flemish and German masters are exhibited in Room 5 where there is a particularly fine "Portrait of a Lady' by Jan van Scorel.

The strongest section of the museum is undoubtedly its 17th century collection spread over rooms 8 to 13, and the Baroque paintings, with more than twenty works by Mattia Preti, are the jewel in the crown. Guido Reni's Bolognese "Christ holding the Cross" and Antoine Le Valentin's "Judith and Holofernes" in Room 8 are particularly fine paintings, as are the four paintings by Matthias Stomer in Room 9, where Melchior Gafa's bozzetti are located. Jusepe de Ribera's tenebrist "St. Francis" and Rosa da Tivoli's (Philip Peter Roos) "Pastoral Scene" in Room 11 are also noteworthy.

Rooms 14 to 17 on the ground floor are devoted to the 18th century. Antoine de Favray dominated 18th century Maltese art and his works are displayed in Room 14, "The Visit" allowing us insight into an 18th century upper class Maltese home. French artists such as Claude Vernet and Pierre Mignard are found in Room 15, whilst Rooms 16 and 17 are devoted to late Italian Baroque artists such as Francesco Solimena and Gian. Domenico Tiepolo. Room 18 has a fine collection of 19th century Italian artists such as Tommaso Minardi and Giuseppe de Nitis, and the Swiss artist Louis Ducros graces Room 19. Rooms 20 to 23 are devoted to Maltese artists of the 17th to the 20th centuries. Notable amongst these are Francesco Fieravino (1620-1680), Francesco Zahra (1710-1773), the Schranz brothers, Giorgio Pullicino (1779-1852), Amedeo Preziosi (1816-1882), Giuseppe Cali (1846-1930), Edward Caruana Dingli (1876-1950), Gianni Vella (1885-1977), Anton Inglott (1915-1945), and Willie Apap (1918-1970). The gesso sculptures of Sciortino are located in Room 7A.

The basement of the museum contains an interesting collection of memorabilia principally from the 18th century. These include maiolica pharmacy jars from the Knights' hospital as well as silverware from the Santo Spirito hospital in Rabat.

THE NATIONAL MUSEUM OF ARCHAEOLOGY

Housed in one of the eight Auberges of the Order in Valletta, the collection in the Auberge de Provence is located in Republic Street. The core of this collection was founded in the early 17th century by G. F. Abela. But it was Sir Themistocles Zammit who organised the collection in systematic chronological order and under whose Directorship much of the present display was acquired.

The Prehistoric collection is concentrated on the ground floor. There is a display of pottery that ranges from the earliest known human settlements on the Islands in the Ghar Dalam period to the late neolithic Tarxien phase. Other artefacts from this time span include tools and personal ornaments. The figurines from Skorba are of particular interest, and there is a reconstruction of a Zebbug phase rock-cut tomb.

The most striking part of the Prehistoric collection is the impressive display of monumental pieces from the Temple period. These include the Tarxien temple spiral reliefs, and large stone slabs with reliefs of processions of

different species of animal, as well as fish representations. All the exhibits in the museum are original pieces, conserved here for their protection and preservation. Copies have been placed on the original site.

From the Temple period there is also the larger than life lower half of a "Mother Goddess" statue found at Tarxien temple, as well as smaller figurines such as the group of seven "Fertility Goddesses" found at Hagar Qim. There is also a showcase of phallic statuettes. Displayed in the innermost room is that icon of Maltese prehistoric art, "The Sleeping Lady", which was discovered in the Hypogeum.

Venus of Malta.

There are also several displays of models of temples showing the evolution of temple architecture.

At the time of writing the Museum is undergoing a major transformation, and the upper floor has not yet been opened to the public. It will contain exhibits from the historic phase of Malta's history, starting with the Phoenician, Punic and Roman periods. These include a wide range of ceramic assemblages and other artefacts recovered from tombs of these periods. The large Phoenician anthropomorphic pottery sarcophagus and the stone candelabrum with bilingual Punic and Greek inscriptions are of particular interest in this section.

It is also intended to enlarge the scope of the old display by including a section on the late Roman/Byzantine and Medieval periods. The upper floor also houses a magnificent numismatic collection.

Phoenician Pottery Anthropomorphic Sarcophagus.

ST. JOHN'S CO-CATHEDRAL

This was the Conventual Church of the Order of St. John. It was built by Girolamo Cassar, and consecrated in 1578, though various structural additions were made up to the middle of the 18th century. Its relatively sombre Mannerist exterior belies the Baroque extravagance of the interior. The high relief bronze of the Saviour on the exterior tympanum attributed to Alessandro Algardi is probably a 19th century substitution.

The barrel vaulted ceiling of the interior was painted between 1662 and 1667, and is the opus magnum of Mattia Preti. It depicts episodes from the life of St. John the Baptist, the patron saint of the Order, as well as saints and heroes of the Order flanking the windows of the vault. The technique used by the artist deserves mention as it was probably unique for the time. Realising the difficulties involved in preparing the

soft Malta limestone for fresco, Mattia Preti primed the porous stone with linseed oil and painted his masterpiece in oil paint over the priming.

The floor of the church is covered by a splendid array of some 400 multicoloured inlaid marble tombstones which are something of a distraction when attending services. They are smothered with heraldic devices, religious and military motifs, and a host of sepulchral symbols such as skulls and father time, and clanking creaking skeletons. Mattia Preti is amongst those entombed in the floor, who represent the flower of European Catholic aristocracy of the 16th to 18th centuries. Preti died in Malta in 1699 at the age of 86.

The oratory is located on the right of the church as one enters and it was erected in 1603. There are three Preti paintings on the ceiling: a

"Crucifixion", an "Ecce Homo", and the "Crowning with Thorns". The oratory contains what is regarded as the most important painting in Malta, namely "The Beheading of St. John" by Michaelangelo Merisi da CARAVAGGIO (1573-1610), one of his last and best works. The signature is writ in blood from the Baptist's dripping neck. I must, however, confess a sneaking preference for Caravaggio's powerful "St. Jerome", also housed in this church.

The side aisles contain the chapels of the various Langues of the Order. The first on the right is that of Castille, Leon and Portugal, and the altarpiece and lunettes are by Mattia Preti. Monuments to two Grandmasters of the Langue are found here: that of Antonio Manoel de Vilhena (1622-1626), in bronze and black marble, and the more subdued memorial to Manoel Pinto de Fonseca (1741-1773), who was the first Grandmaster to assume the title of Most Serene Highness. Hence the closed crown which surmounts his coat of arms.

Beyond this chapel is the entrance to the cemetery which contains the relics of those who fell in the Great Siege, and which were transferred here from Fort St. Angelo when the church was built.

The next chapel is that of Aragon and it contains the splendid altarpiece of "St. George" in lustrous colours. It is the earliest work by Mattia Preti in Malta, who in fact painted it in Naples and sent it here as an example of his work

when soliciting for the commission to paint the church vault. The other paintings in this chapel are examples of the artist's later work. There are four lavishly decorated sepulchral monuments to Grandmasters Nicolas Cotoner (1668-1680), Ramon Perellos (1697-1720), Martin de Redin (1657-1660) and Rafael Cotoner (1660-1663). The first two are particularly magnificent examples of Italian baroque sculpture, that of Perellos being by Giuseppe Mazzuoli.

St. John's Co-Cathedral.

The chapel of Auvergne follows, and it contains the monument to Grandmaster Annet de Clermont de Chatte-Gessan who died four months after his election in 1660.

At the end of the right aisle is the Chapel of the Blessed Sacrament which formerly held the icon of the Madonna of Philermos brought over by the Knights from Rhodes. This icon, together with the alleged relic of the right hand of St. John the Baptist was one of the few

items carried away by Grandmaster von Hompesch on his expulsion from the Islands. The relic is now untraceable. The famous silver gates protect this chapel. They are reputed to been painted black in 1798 to avoid the attention of Napoleon's looting troops.

The high altar in the elevated chancel is a delight of lapus lazuli and other precious stones embellished with gilt metal reliefs. The carved wooden choirstalls and lectern behing the altar are amongst the oldest fixtures in the church. Dominating the back of the Choir, indeed the whole church, is the colossal marble "Baptism of Christ". The work was entrusted to Melchior Gafa', but on his untimely death it was executed by Giuseppe Mazzuoli.

The chapel of the Holy Relics is situated at the far end of the left aisle, and the newly formed Anglo-Bavarian Langue was installed here in 1784. It contains a wooden figure of St. John from the poop of the enormous "Gran Caracca", a vessel in which the Knights sailed out of Rhodes.

The Chapel of Provence follows and it contains the monuments of Grandmasters Antoine de Paule (1623-1636) and Jean Paul Lascaris Castellar (1636-1657). Steps in a corner of this chapel lead down to the crypt of the early Grandmasters. Buried here are Grandmasters Phillip Villiers de l'Isle Adam (1521-1534, whose tomb by Antonello Cagini was

St. John's Co-Cathedral.

transferred here from Fort St. Angelo in 1577), Jean Parisot de La Valette (1557-1568), Jean Levesque de la Cassiere (1572-1581, founder of the church and of most of Valletta's important buildings), Cardinal Hugues de Verdalle, Pierino del Monte, Aloph de Wignacourt, Martin Garzes, Luis Mendes de Vasconcellos, Juan d'Homedes, Pietro del Ponte and Claude de la Sengle. Although no inscription records the fact, Francisco Ximenes de Texada is also buried here. The only resident of the crypt who was not a Grandmaster is the English secretary of La Valette, Sir Oliver Starkey, Turcopilier of the Langue of England.

The Chapel of France is west of that of Provence, and it underwent some "redecoration" in the Nazarener zeal of the 1840's. Buried here are Grandmasters Adrian de Wignacourt (1690-1697) and Emanuel de Rohan-Polduc (1775-1797). This chapel is unusual in that it commemorates two men who were not Grandmasters. The first is Jacques de Wignacourt, brother of the Grandmaster, who died on a visit to Malta in 1615, and whose commemorative white urn appears to be the earliest funerary monument in the upper church. The other is Louis Charles d'Orleans, Count of Beaujolais, and brother of King Louis Philippe of France, who died in 1808. His memorial by the celebrated Jean Jacques Pradier is the last of the funerary monuments in the church. The reclining figure is a tour de force of neo-classical sculpture; the only instance of this style in the otherwise supremely baroque interior. The neo-classical relief background is by Fortin.

The Chapel of Italy adjoins, and it contains a richly decorated marble altar, as well as Mattia Preti's masterful "Mystic Marriage of St. Catherine". Grandmaster Gregorio Carafa (1680-1690) is buried here and the monument contains his imposing bronze baroque bust portrait.
The most westerly of the chapels

on the left aisle is that of the German Langue. It contains paintings by the Maltese artist Stefano Erardi. To the left of the main door entrance is the bronze and black marble mausoleum of Grandmaster Marcantonio Zondadari (1720-1722).

During the month of June a glorious set of Flemish tapestries by Judocus de Vos is hung in the church. There are fourteen large panels in colour and as many smaller ones in grisaille, mostly after paintings by Rubens and Poussin. These are normally exhibited in the adjoining Cathedral

Museum, which also contains other church memorabilia such as vestments, chalices, illuminated books, monstrances and other relics.

One cannot also fail to mention the intricate painted sculptured designs with which the walls of the church are smothered, which were designed by Mattia Preti himself.

Chapel of France.

THE GRANDMASTER'S PALACE

Originally planned to be built on the site of the Auberge de Castille, the Magisterial Palace was the official residence of the Grandmasters, then of the British Governors, and now it houses the Maltese Parliament. The exterior is unimpressive. It contains two interconnecting courtyards, the larger of which is known as Neptune's courtyard because of the bronze statue transferred here from the Neptune's fountain in the old fishmarket at the Marina. Prince Alfred's courtyard contains Pinto's 1745 clock whose four dials indicate the time, the day, the month and the phases of the

moon. Figures in Turkish costume ritually strike the hour at the top of the clock tower. The ground floor was originally used for stables, stores and service quarters, and nowadays is occupied by various Government offices.

The first floor or 'piano nobile' is reached by a staircase of shallow steps, said to be so constructed as to allow the easy ascent of Knights burdened with heavy armour. The right hand passage leads to the House of Representatives, and the Armoury corridor gives entrance to the Council or Tapestry Chamber. This room was used as the Council

Hall of the Order, and from 1921-1974 for sittings of the Malta Legislative Assembly.
This striking room contains a priceless set of Gobelins tapestries presented to the Palace by Grandmaster Perellos on taking office.
There are ten large tapestries which form part of a series known as the "Indian Hangings", or Les Tenture des Indes, depicting the flora and fauna of three continents in astonishing detail and in exquisite colour.
The ceiling is coffered and painted, and has finely carved wooden rafters.

The Grandmaster's palace, Valletta.

The Grandmaster's palace, Valletta.

Beyond the Dining Room is what was known as the Supreme Council Chamber Room, and known also as the Throne Room or the Hall of St. Michael and St. George. The ceiling is also splendidly coffered, but the tour de force of this room is the frescoed frieze depicting twelve episodes from the Great Siege by Matteo Perez D'Aleccio. They were painted within a few years of the episode under guidance of eyewitness accounts. The wooden minstrels' gallery is said to have been part of the Gran Caracca which sailed out of Rhodes in 1523.

The Ambassador's Room contains many portraits, mostly of foreign dignitaries, and a frieze depicting episodes from the history of the Order between 1309 and 1524. The Yellow or Page's Room contains two paintings by Jusepe de Ribera

The Grandmaster's palace, Neptune's Courtyard.

"lo Spagnoletto", as well as a frieze depicting episodes from the history of the Order between 1221 and 1291.

The Palace Armoury has been sadly depleted over the centuries, yet it still contains a remarkable collection of old suits of armour and weapons pertaining to the period of the Order. The Renaissance Knight, when clad head to toe, carried at least twenty five pieces of armour, and a few such complete suits of armour are exhibited in the museum. Of particular note is that made for Grandmaster Garzes at the end of the 16th century, and the 17th century full suit of armour made for Aloph de Wignacourt which is lavishly engraved and decorated with gold damascening. Other than various types of weaponry manufactured in Europe, there are also showcases exhibiting weapons of war captured from the Muslim foe.

The Grandmaster's palace.

Tapestry in Grandmaster's palace.

The Grandmaster's palace, Pinto's clock.

The Grandmaster's palace.

The Palace Armoury.

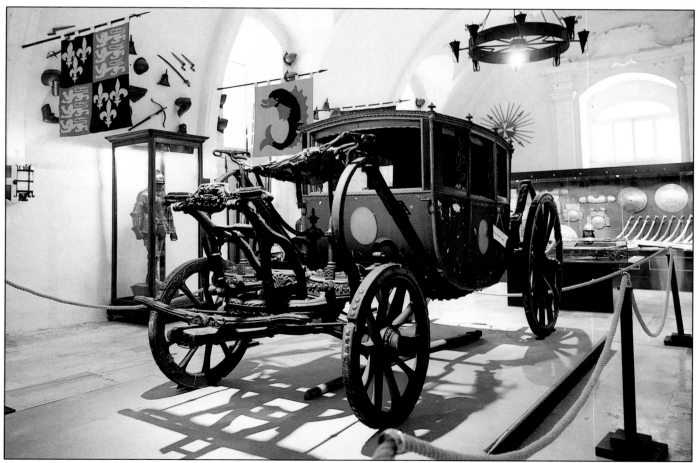

CASA ROCCA PICCOLA

Situated at 161 Republic Street, this is a must for all those interested in seeing the interior of a well-to-do Maltese home of the 18th century. It is a home rather than a museum, and the Baron and his family still reside there.

Period furniture, paintings, porcelain, costume, lace, chess sets, parasols and all the bric-a-brac of the time are on show.

THE NATIONAL WAR MUSEUM

This is one of the most popular museums, and it is housed in Fort St. Elmo at the tip of Valletta. It is the site of epic battles in Malta's two Great Sieges, and where six Maltese soldiers lost their lives on the first day of action in the Second World War.

The collection in this gem of a 16th century fort encompasses war memorabilia from the French and British periods (the period of the Order of St. John is covered by the "Palace Armoury" museum).

Most of the exhibits, however, pertain to the Second World War. Among the principal items in the Main Hall are two World War I German torpedoes and another of Austrian origin, an Austro-Hungarian World War I "Minewerfer", an Italian Breda 47mm anti-tank gun, an American naval searchlight and a British 90cm anti-aircraft searchlight.

There is also an Italian Vickers Terni 75mm field gun, and General Eisenhower's Willys Jeep "Husky". Pride of place goes to the Gloster

The George Cross.

The National War Museum.

Gladiator aircraft "Faith".
It is ironic that although the museum contains exhibits of enemy sea and aircraft, there is scarce a relic of any of our guns which actually shot them down in battle. These were dismantled in the 1960's and cut up and sold for a pittance as scrap iron.
The museum houses a complete E-Boat that took part in the abortive Italian attack on Grand Harbour below St. Elmo on 26th July 1941. It was captured after it had strayed from the main scene of action.

The numerous photographs on the walls of the main hall depict the conditions prevailing in wartime Malta.
They show the extent of the war damage and the primitive living quarters in underground shelters. Other items include a collection of small arms, gas masks and steel helmets, as well as a selection of wartime ration cards and other documents.

A section is devoted to the Royal

and Merchant navies which includes relics from the "Ohio".

There are also exhibits from the aerial combat which include the front section of a Spitfire and the wing of a Messerschnitt 109.
For those interested in the Second World War, a replica of the War Operations Room can be visited at a separate location in Lascaris Ditch, within the bastions.

War operations room.

Fort St. Elmo.

RABAT

THE MUSEUM OF ROMAN ANTIQUITIES

Located just outside Mdina and sited in a 1st century B.C. Roman town house, this museum contains artefacts from the Roman period. The house itself contains elegant mosaics and high quality marble Roman sculptures. Ceramic, glass, metal and bone artefacts, principally from Roman tombs, are displayed. There is also an impressive olive pipper from a Roman villa. An annexe contains a large collection of Muslim stelae from the Arab cemetery excavated on this site.

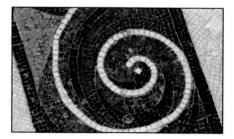

ST. PAUL'S GROTTO

This is located in the heart of Rabat next door to St. Paul's Church. St. Paul is reputed to have sheltered here whilst in Malta, and stone from the cave was accorded miraculous powers.

THE WIGNACOURT MUSEUM

This museum is situated opposite St. Paul's Grotto, and up to the late 19th century provided the only access to the Grotto; Nelson visited the Grotto in May 1800 via this building. Displayed in the museum are over 150 paintings, ecclesiastical furniture, embroidered vestments, several sculptures, an archaeological collection, and a number of maps, books and coins. The emphasis is on the ecclesiastic, and the Maltése artist.

St. Paul's and St. Agatha's Catacombs

These are a must to visit, and in summertime offer a cool repose from the sun. There are pagan, Jewish and Christian catacombs with a wide variety of tomb types among the maze of passageways. Note particularly the agape tables or triclinia; round tables hewn out of the rock where commemorative feasts were thought to be held on death anniversaries.

St. Agatha's Museum

Just up the road from the above complex, this museum contains a fascinating collection of geological, prehistoric, classical and medieval artefacts. Below there is an intricate maze of catacombs with interesting palaeo-christian wall frescoes. In the medieval period a section of these catacombs was converted into a rock-cut church, and it is adorned with frescoes of standing saints. The genial curator will be happy to show you around.

MDINA

The "Silent City" is best seen on foot. Try to extricate yourself from tourist groups and discover the side streets. Don't miss the spectacular view from Bastion Square at the tip of the city. The Cathedral is by Lorenzo Gafa', and it replaced the old church damaged in the 1693 earthquake. Next door is the Cathedral Museum, which houses artefacts salvaged from the old church, such as the 15th century wooden choirstalls. It contains a fine collection of paintings with most of the major schools of the 16th to 18th centuries being represented.

The early 15th century large tempera retable of St. Paul from the old church is particularly notable. This polyptych is made up of a large central panel of St. Paul surrounded by eight smaller panels.

The museum also boasts a fine coin collection.

Another museum in Mdina housed in a splendid building is the Museum of Natural History in Vilhena Palace, just inside the main gate. But most of all in Mdina, wander the streets and admire the old aristocratic palaces and houses, and look into the numerous churches.

Cathedral Museum, Mdina.

Cathedral museum Chapel.

Mdina.

Maritime museum and St. Lawrence Church.

Maritime Museum.

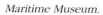

BIRGU (VITTORIOSA)

Don't overlook the cities on the other side of Grand Harbour to Valletta. Birgu was the old headquarters of the Order and is steeped in history. The original Knights' Auberges were located here. See if you can discover the Auberge of England and the old Inquisitor's Palace, which is being converted into a Museum of Ethnography. There is a fascinating little museum round the corner from St. Lawrence Church where you can see La Valette's hat and sword. On the waterfront there is an immaculate Maritime Museum housed in the 19th century Naval Bakery. All manner of artefacts associated with seafaring are to be found here, both from the time of the Order and from the British period. Old nautical instruments, ships' doctor's equipment, portolani, log books, maps, costumes, anchors, ship models, engines and paintings are just a few examples of the maritime miscellanea to be found here. The waterfront area is scheduled for a massive redevelopment in the near future, and there will be a yacht marina, cafes, and other attractions.

GHAR DALAM MUSEUM

G   har Dalam lies in the south east of Malta, on the side of the valley leading down to Birzebbuga. This cave was formed in the Pleistocene period (Ice Ages) within the lower coralline limestone layer, and it is Malta's most important palaeontological site. It contains a sequence of fossilised deposits of animals extending back from the Pleistocene period (130,000 years ago) down to modern times.

One can visit both the cave and museum, where examples of the fossilised bones of several types of Maltese pygmy elephants, dwarf hippopotami and of other species are displayed. In the cave itself, which is some 145 metres long, stalactities and stalagmites abound.

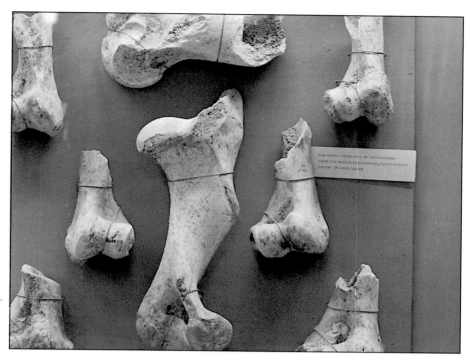

ARCHAEOLOGICAL SITES

BORG-IN-NADUR

On the other side of the valley from the Għar Dalam Cave, and further down towards the sea, is this Bronze Age site.

It is not easy to find, but worth the effort to see Malta's only example of Bronze Age fortifications. Close by is the remains of an earlier Temple period building, and in the rocks on the sea shore below this site you can discover some half submerged Bronze Age silo pits and cart tracks.

THE HAĠAR QIM AND MNAJDRA TEMPLE COMPLEXES

These are situated in a commanding position over the cliffs of the south east part of Malta beyond the village of Qrendi. They are among the best preserved of the temples in Malta, along with that of Tarxien, and both sites are a must for any visitor to Malta. Sun and sea and beaches can be found anywhere, but prehistoric temples like these can only be seen in Malta.

Ħaġar Qim is a complex of temples, with additions added on as the temple period developed. It is built exclusively from the surrounding globigerina limestone, and the well dressed stones of its facade contrast with the irregular megaliths of Ġgantija in Gozo. The apse beyond the two pedestalled altars produced the famous "Fat Lady" figurines which can be seen in the National Museum of Archaeology. The outer wall on the eastern side contains a gargantuan block of stone 7 metres long and weighing about 20 tons. It is the largest recorded from a Maltese temple.

Mnajdra is situated about 500 metres beyond Ħaġar Qim, from where there is a sweeping view of the island of Filfla. As with Ħaġar Qim, it is a complex multi-temple site.

The middle temple was the last to be built in the Tarxien phase, and it has a four apse and niche plan. The small temple on the right has a trefoil plan and was built in the earlier Ġgantija phase. The third temple (second in date) was built in the early Tarxien phase and the sophistication of its workmanship makes it probably the finest of all surviving temples. Megaliths in this temple are decorated with close-spaced pitting, probably produced with some form of drill. The corbelling effect, whereby the upper courses of stone draw inwards, (towards a possible ceiling), is well demonstrated in this temple.

Ħaġar Qim Temple Complex.

Ħaġar Qim, window.

Ħaġar Qim, entrance.

Ħaġar Qim complex.

Mnajdra.

Mnajdra with Filfla in the background.

Pitted decoration in Mnajdra Temple.

hese were discovered in 1914 when a farmer was encountering difficulty ploughing his field because of large blocks of stone. The site was excavated by Sir Temi Zammit between 1915 and 1917, and it was revealed to be a multi-temple site.

Entering through the concave facade of the south temple, which has a four apse plan, it is evident that there has been some restoration work. This has been done in such a way that it cannot be confused with the original. The relief carvings also are copies, the originals being preserved in the National Museum of Archaeology. In the first right apse is the waist high remains of a giant "Mother Goddess" statue that stood some 2.75 metres high, and in the apse opposite is a block with animal friezes.

Going through to the second or central temple, one notices that it is unique in that it is the only temple in Malta with a six apse plan. There are giant bowls in the courtyards, and some reddening of the stones due to fire. A doorway through the first right hand apse leads to a chamber which has two particularly interesting carved blocks. The first has the relief of a bull, and the second larger 5 metre block has two reliefs, another bull above and a sow with suckling piglets below.

The east temple is smaller and belongs to the same early phase as the south temple. It was somewhat damaged when the central temple was built.

Further east are the remains of a smaller fourth temple, belonging to the earliest Ġgantija phase.

THE HYPOGEUM

Described in the text, the Hypogeum is in Paola, not far from the Tarxien temples. It is an impressive UNESCO World Heritage site that should not be missed. In recent years the site has been closed as it has undergone an extensive UNESCO aided conservation programme. By the time this book reaches you it should have reopened, and there will be a new visitor's centre comprising a permanent exhibition and an audio-visual presentation.

ROMAN BATHS AND SAN PAWL MILQGHI

The Roman remains at Għajn Tuffieħa are an example of a residential country villa of Roman times, whereas those at San Pawl Milqgħi (Burmarrad) are more of an agricultural nature with well preserved remains of the apparatus for extracting oil from olives.

Mosaic, Roman Villa at Għajn Tuffieħa.

Roman Villa, Għajn Tuffieħa.

GOZO

Make sure you visit Gozo. The drive and the ferry crossing are a pleasant experience in themselves, and this smaller island is a little more picturesque, greener and leisurely than Malta.

The cathedral in the old citadel has a trompe l'oeil dome. Next door is the Archaeological Museum which contains artefacts uncovered in Gozo and Comino. The ground floor is devoted to prehistory, the room to the right of the entrance being entirely dedicated to finds from the Ġgantija temples. There is a large stone slab with a relief carving of a snake, and fragments

The Gozo Archaeological Museum.

Gozo, Cathedral.

of painted plaster which appeared to cover the interior of the temple walls. A shard of pottery shows birds in flight. The upper floor is devoted to the historical Phoenician, Roman and Medieval periods. There is a room full of anchors and amphorae from Roman wrecks, and an interesting collection of ceramic and glass cremation urns. The famous Maimuna tombstone in beautiful Arabic script is also on the upper floor.

Other museums in the old citadel include the Cathedral Museum, a Folk Museum and a Natural History Museum; one can also visit the old dungeons.

The Ġgantija temples in Xaghra are a complex of two temples both built in the Ġgantija phase. That on the left is the older and is a five apsed temple, whereas on the right one finds a four apsed niche temple. The gargantuan irregular coralline limestone megaliths of the exterior walls contrast with the smaller better dressed blocks of the interior. The boundary wall is probably the most striking part of these Ġgantija temples. Take a

Gozo, Folklore Museum.

Altar Niche in Ġgantija Temples.

walk around them. Regretfully the Brochtorff Circle close by is not open to the public. Within the village of Xaghra itself there is a delightful Toy Museum.

In the village of Gharb in the church square there is a fascinating Folk Museum displayed in an old village house. All manner of bygone crafts and implements are on show here. The village church itself is a gem of Baroque architecture.

Ġgantija Temple.

Gozo Archaeology Museum, Glass Cremation Urn.

Gozo Archaeology Museum, Lead Anchors.

Gozo, Menhir.

Gozo Archaeology Museum, Amphorae.

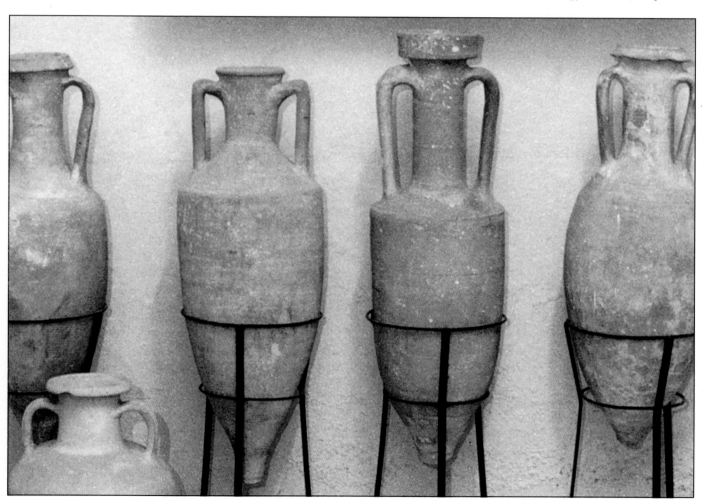

SELECT CHRONOLOGICAL BIBLIOGRAPHY

Zammit Maempel G. 1977 **An Outline of Maltese Geology** The Author, Malta

Zammit Maempel G. 1987 **Għar Dalam Cave and Deposits** The Author, Malta

Evans J. D. 1971 **The Prehistoric Antiquities of the Maltese Islands** The Athlone Press, London

Bonanno A. 1986 **An Illustrated Guide to Prehistoric Gozo** Gaulitana 3, Gozo

Trump D. 1972 **Malta: An Archaeological Guide** Faber and Faber Ltd, London

Gouder T. 1991 **Malta and the Phoenicians** in "Lombard Bank (Malta) Ltd. Annual Report"

Bonanno A. 1992 **Roman Malta** World Confederation of Salesian Past Pupils of Don Bosco, Italy

Buhagiar M. 1992 **The Maltese Palaeochristian Hypogea** in "Collected Papers", University of Malta

Luttrell A. T. (Ed.) 1975 **Medieval Malta** The British School at Rome, London

Brown T. S. 1975 **Byzantine Malta** in Luttrell A. T. "Medieval Malta"

Wettinger G. 1986 **The Arabs in Malta** in "Malta. Studies of its Heritage and History", Mid-Med Bank Ltd, Malta

Brincat J. M. 1991 **Malta 870 - 1054 Al-Himyari's Account** Said Int. Ltd, Malta

Schermerhorn E. W. 1929 **Malta of the Knights** W. H. Heinemann Ltd, U.K.

Testa C. 1997 **The French in Malta** Midsea Books Ltd, Malta

Mallia-Milanes V. (Ed.) 1988 **The British Colonial Experience 1800-1964** Mireva Publications, Malta

Vella P. 1985 **Malta: Blitzed But Not Beaten** Progress Press Co. Ltd, Malta

Frendo H. 1989 **Malta's Quest for Independence** Valletta Publishing and Promotion Co. Ltd, Malta

Cremona J. J. 1994 **The Maltese Constitution and Constitutional History since 1813** P.E.G. Ltd, Malta

Blouet B. 1972 **The Story of Malta** Faber and Faber Ltd, London (the best general account)